THE AMERICAN SIGN LANGUAGE PHRASE BOOK

LOU FANT

ILLUSTRATIONS BY BETTY G. MILLER

Contemporary Books, Inc.
Chicago

Library of Congress Cataloging in Publication Data

Fant, Louie J.
    The American sign language phrase book.

    Includes index.
    1. Sign language—Dictionaries.   I. Miller, Betty G.
II. Title.
HV2475.F36   1983   419   83-15435
ISBN 0-8092-5507-3

Published by Contemporary Books, Inc.
180 North Michigan Avenue, Chicago, Illinois 60601
Manufactured in the United States of America
Library of Congress Catalog Card Number: 83-15435
International Standard Book Number: 0-8092-5507-3

Published simultaneously in Canada by Beaverbooks, Ltd.
195 Allstate Parkway, Valleywood Business Park
Markham, Ontario L3R 4T8, Canada

Contents

6. HEALTH

How do you feel? . . . Do you feel all right? . . . I don't feel well . . . Where does it hurt? . . . My stomach is upset . . . I have a cold . . . My nose is runny . . . My head aches . . . I have a toothache/stomachache . . . I need a dentist/doctor . . . Do you have any aspirin? . . . I've run out of medicine . . . I have to buy some medicine . . . I have to take pills . . . You need to have an x-ray . . . It's time to take your temperature . . . You have to have a shot . . . I feel better now . . . I was in bed for two weeks . . . Were any bones broken? . . . You lost a lot of blood . . . They have to draw some blood . . . Have you ever had a tooth pulled? . . . I had a physical last week . . . My husband had an operation . . . My wife is in the hospital . . . My father passed away last month . . . Call the ambulance . . . I have an appointment at 2:30 . . . Where's my toothbrush? . . . I want to brush my teeth . . . I already took a bath/shower . . . Wash your hands/face . . . I haven't shaved yet . . . May I borrow your hair dryer? . . . Brush your hair . . . I lost my comb . . . Do you have hospitalization insurance?

7. WEATHER

It's beautiful today . . . The sun is hot . . . I enjoy sitting in the sun . . . It was cold this morning . . . It will freeze tonight . . . Maybe it will snow tomorrow . . . There was thunder and lightning last night . . . It rained yesterday . . . Do you have a raincoat? . . . I lost my umbrella . . . Where are your galoshes/rubbers? . . . It's windy today . . . Yesterday evening at sunset, the clouds were beautiful . . . I hope it clears up this afternoon . . . I like spring/aummer/autumn/winter best . . . You have to have chains to drive in the mountains in winter . . . I'm afraid of tornados . . . What's the temperature? . . . Has the snow melted? . . . There was a flood last year . . . The temperature is below zero . . . Have you ever been in an earthquake?

8. FAMILY

Your father is nice looking . . . You look like your mother . . . My brother is younger than I . . . My sister speaks several languages fluently . . . His son wants to be an astronaut . . . Her daughter works here . . . My uncle is a farmer . . . My aunt lives in town . . . Your nephew gave me a book . . . His niece will help you . . . Her grandfather gave her grandmother a book . . . My cousin is a pilot . . . Who is that man? . . . Did you see the woman? . . . The baby is cute . . . The girl told the boy that she loves him . . . Father told the little boy to play outside . . . The girl's doll is broken . . . How many children are coming? . . . Our family is large/small . . . We had a family reunion last summer . . . We met at Grandfather's farm

9. SCHOOL

Do you go to school? . . . I go to college . . . I'm majoring in English . . . What course are you taking this semester? . . . I'm a student . . . I graduated last year . . . I'm in graduate school now . . . I like to study . . . Where's the administration building? . . . You've got to go to the library and do some research . . . I got an "A" on my paper . . . I studied all night . . . Where's my pocket calculator? . . . I loaned out my typewriter . . . My roommate can't sleep while I'm typing . . . I have a question . . . Did you ask him? . . . The teacher asked me a lot of questions . . . No talking during the test . . . We have a test tomorrow . . . Close/open your books . . . Begin/stop writing . . . I lost my pencil . . . Your writing is terrible . . . Please don't erase the board . . . Did you pass or fail? . . . Any questions? . . . You haven't turned in your paper to me yet . . . She and I discussed it . . . Let's take a break . . . When you've been absent, you must bring an excuse . . . Additional vocabulary words

1

How to Use This Book

American Sign Language, commonly abbreviated to ASL and also known as Ameslan, is the sign language most deaf people use when they are communicating among themselves. It has its own grammatical structure, which differs from English grammar. You must approach ASL in the same manner you would approach any foreign language—do not expect ASL to be like English or to conform to rules of English grammar. *Do not ask why ASL, or any language, has a certain structure; ask only how it works. It does no good at all to ask Spanish-speaking people, for example, why they put adjectives after nouns; they just do, and you must accept that. Some of the constructions in ASL may seem odd to you at first because they depart radically from the way we say things in English, but after a while they will seem as natural as English.

It is a common misconception that ASL is merely the finger-spelling of English words. Fingerspelling—using the manual al-

---

*For a more detailed discussion of the grammatical structure of ASL, see Chapter 2, "A Guide to Ameslan."

1

phabet to spell out entire words letter by letter—is occasionally incorporated into ASL, but the vocabulary of ASL consists of signs. (See the Appendix for a complete treatment of this manual alphabet.)

The format of this book is not that of a traditional foreign language textbook. There are no formal grammatical exercises or drills, and there are no vocabulary lists to memorize. Rather, this book is a guide to conversation with deaf people. It contains phrases, expressions, sentences, and questions that come up in casual, everyday conversations. These phrases enable you to begin talking with deaf people without first having to master the grammar of the language.

Chapter 2, entitled "A Guide to ASL," covers the major components of ASL grammar. It is not a complete grammar of ASL. It is intended to help you better understand the structure of the sentences in this book, but it is not necessary that you understand the grammatical structure before you begin signing those sentences. In other words, you may skip over the chapter on grammar and go directly to the sentences and begin signing. As you become more proficient in ASL, you will want to create your own sentences, and then you will need to study the ASL guide. At this stage, the Dictionary/Index will also be helpful to you in locating the signs you want to use in your own expressions.

Chapters 3 through 17 cover the basic topics that occur in the ordinary course of our lives. (The chapter on health also includes some expressions that are needed in emergency situations.) These 15 chapters are self-contained and do not need to be employed in any particular order. You may begin wherever you like, choosing whichever subject you wish, and be able to proceed without having read the previous chapters. If you are seeking quick access to the rudiments of language for your first conversation with a deaf person, though, the chapters entitled "Everyday Expressions," "Signing and Deafness," and "Getting Acquainted" might be the best ones to begin with.

This book can be used not only as an instant reference manual, but also as a study guide should you wish to become fluent in ASL. If you do wish to assimilate the phrases, the most efficient way to use this book is to study one chapter thoroughly, practicing the sentences until you can do them without looking at the pictures. The next step is to use them immediately in conversation. This will help fix them in your memory. To become fluent in ASL, it is important to study and converse in a regular, consistent manner. Do not be afraid of making mistakes, for everyone errs while learning a new language. Deaf people do not expect perfection and usually will cheerfully help you correct your errors.

SIGN LABELS

To enable us to talk about the signs of ASL each sign has been given a name, or label. We use English words for these labels. In this book the labels appear beneath the picture of the sign. People often confuse the meaning of a sign with its label, but a sign may have several meanings and the label is only one of its meanings. English labels for signs merely provide us with a convenient way of designating which sign we want to talk about or which sign to use.

Let's look at an example. The word *run* has numerous meanings in English. Some of them are:

He *runs* fast.
My nose *runs*.
There's a *run* on the stock market
She's *running* for office.
He scored a *run*.
You stocking has a *run* in it.

Figure 1. RUN

The sign labeled RUN (Figure 1) could be used only in the first example above, for that is the only meaning of that sign. Each of the other examples requires a different sign.

A sign label does not tell you how a sign may be used to express meanings quite different from the label. Take for example the sign FINISH (Figures 2, 3).

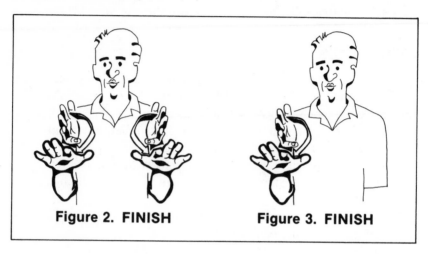

Figure 2. FINISH   **Figure 3. FINISH**

The sign phrase EAT FINISH may mean: (1) ate, eaten; (2) already eat, already eaten; (3) did eat; or (4) done eating (Figures 4, 5).

Figure 4. EAT   **Figure 5. FINISH**

In this signed sentence, WORK FINISH GO TO HOME (Figures 6–9), the FINISH sign indicates that when one act is over, another follows. This sentence would translate as "After work I am going home," "After work I went home," or "When work is done, I am going home."

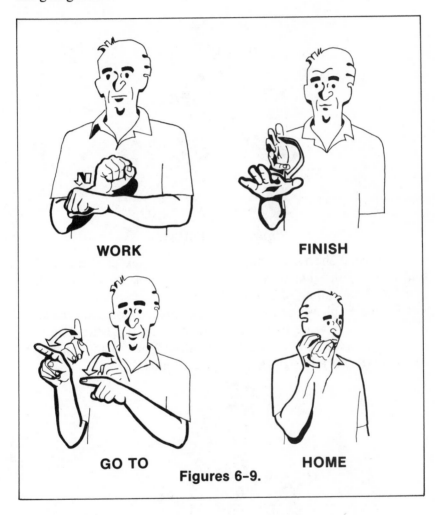

WORK   FINISH

GO TO   HOME

Figures 6–9.

One form of the FINISH sign by itself can mean "That's enough!," "Stop it!," or "I/She/He did already!" (Figure 10).

The FINISH sign offers an excellent example of the danger of confusing a sign label with the meaning of the sign. Obviously this sign means much more than merely "finish."

Figure 10. FINISH!

When using the Dictionary/Index at the back of this book to find a sign you want to use, be sure you look for the sign that matches the meaning of the word you have in mind. Do not look just for the English word itself. For example, if you want the sign for "run" in the sense that someone is running for office, you will have to think of "competing," "contesting," or "racing" in order to locate the correct sign (COMPETE, Figure 11).

Figure 11. COMPETE

READING THE DRAWINGS

The pictures are to be read from left to right when they are read as a sentence. However, an individual sign may sometimes require more than one picture to illustrate it, and will sometimes be read from right to left. Five types of aids are provided to help you know which way to read a drawing, and thus form the sign correctly.

The Five Aids for Reading the Drawings

The first aid is the use of both *bold* (dark-lined) and *light-lined* drawings. The bold-lined drawings show the final position of the sign. The light-lined drawings show the first and, if necessary, additional positions of the sign. In the sign labeled DELICIOUS (Figure 12), for example, the light-lined drawing shows the middle finger touching the lips. The bold-lined drawing shows the hand turned outward. These are the first and final positions, respectively. Always remember that the bold-lined drawing shows the final position of the sign.

Figure 12. DELICIOUS   **Figure 13. DAY**

The second aid is the use of several kinds of *arrows*, which show exactly how the hands move in forming a sign. The sign DAY (Figure 13), for example, is formed by moving the arm from the first position (light-lined) to the final position (bold-lined), following the movement indicated by the arrow.

Repetitive movement is shown by the use of a bent arrow, as in the signs HAPPY (Figure 14) and FOOTBALL (Figure 15). This means you do the same movement twice.

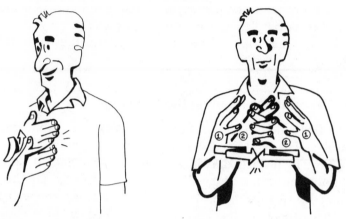

Figure 14. HAPPY   **Figure 15. FOOTBALL**

Swerving movement is shown by a twisted arrow, as in the sign labeled NEVER (Figure 16).

Figure 16. NEVER

Circular movement is shown by a circular arrow, as in the signs COFFEE (Figure 17) and GOING (Figure 18).

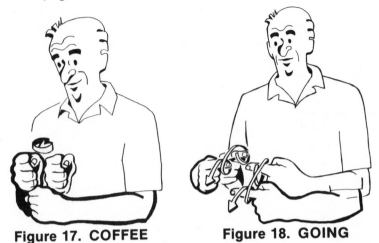

Figure 17. COFFEE   **Figure 18. GOING**

The arrows in the sign CAR (Figure 19) show the hands repeating a movement, but in opposite directions. The sign looks as if you were steering a car.

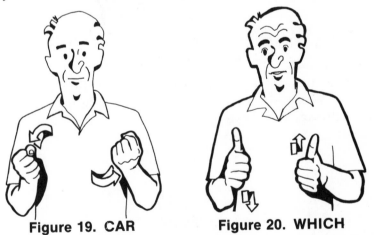

Figure 19. CAR   **Figure 20. WHICH**

In the sign WHICH (Figure 20), the arrows indicate that the hands move alternately. As the left hand goes up, the right hand goes down. Then both hands reverse their directions (left: down; right: up), then they reverse again going in their original directions.

The same thing applies to the sign CONTROL (Figure 21) as does to the WHICH sign, but *numbers*, the third aid, have been added to help you see more clearly where the hands begin and end. When both hands are in their number one positions, the right hand is farther out from the chest than the left. The arrows show that the right hand moves backward, and the left hand moves forward, reversing their positions. The arrows then show that the hands reverse positions again as the hands move to the third position. (Note that both the first and third positions are shown in bold-lines since that is the final, as well as the beginning, position. This will occur only rarely, but if in doubt, look at the numbers. The sign looks as if you are guiding a horse with the reins.

Figure 21. CONTROL

The arrows together with the numbers in Figure 22 (HAMBURGER) show a reversal of position here. In the first position the right hand is on top, and in the second position it is on bottom.

Figure 22. HAMBURGER

A *broken arrow*, the fourth aid, is shown in Figure 23 (TREES) along with the circular arrows that show how the hand moves from first to final position. The broken arrow means that there may be two or three repetitions of the sign. The sign is repeated (third and fourth positions) only once in the drawing.

Figure 23. TREES

The *squiggles* in Figure 24 (WAIT) are the fifth aid, and they tell you to wriggle the fingers. In the sign for "13" (Figure 25), they tell you to wriggle the index and second finger together, but not the rest of the hand.

Figure 24. WAIT

Figure 25. 13

The Angle of the Pictures

In most of the drawings the signer is shown facing directly front, but many signs can best be learned by seeing the sign from an angle slightly off center; thus, the signer is sometimes shown facing slightly to his right or to his left. The WANT sign (Figure 26), for instance, would be difficult to read if it were shown

Figure 26. WANT

straight on, so the signer is shown facing slightly to his right to give you a clearer view of the sign. When you make the sign, however, do not turn to your right, but make it straight toward the person to whom you are signing. In a few of the drawings, such as those for LESSON (Figures 27 and 28), the signer is shown from a rear view, as well as from the front, to help you to see the sign more clearly.

Figure 27. LESSON   **Figure 28. LESSON (rear view)**

Labeling of the Drawings

When more than one drawing is required to illustrate how a single sign is made, each sign label is followed by a number. For example, the illustration of the sign AWFUL requires two steps, and these are labeled "AWFUL (1)," and "AWFUL (2):"

AWFUL (1)   **AWFUL (2)**

When a single concept can be signed in more than one way, several possible signs are shown, and their labels are followed by a letter. For example, the three separate ways to sign BAPTIZE are labeled "BAPTIZE (A)," "BAPTIZE (B)," and "BAPTIZE (C):"

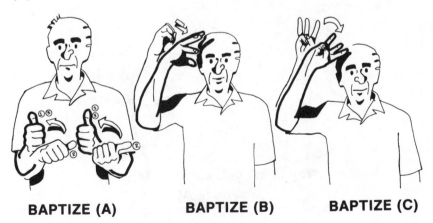

BAPTIZE (A)   **BAPTIZE (B)**   **BAPTIZE (C)**

Sometimes, an entire phrase or sentence can be said in more than one way. In these cases, each sentence, along with its component signs, is shown and indicated with a letter. For example, the sentence "Why didn't you eat last night?" can be signed as "PAST NIGHT YOU EAT NOT WHY" or as "PAST NIGHT WHY YOU EAT NOT:"

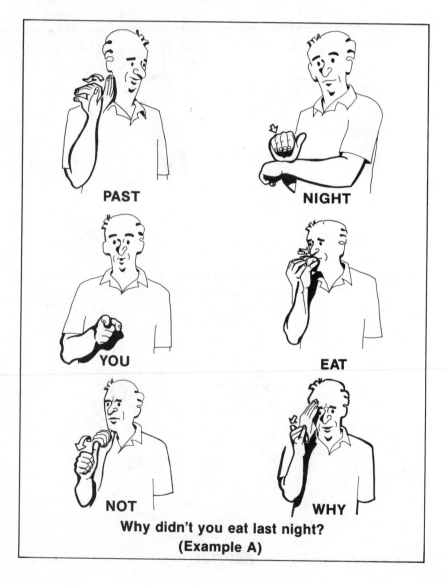

PAST

NIGHT

YOU

EAT

NOT

WHY

Why didn't you eat last night?
(Example A)

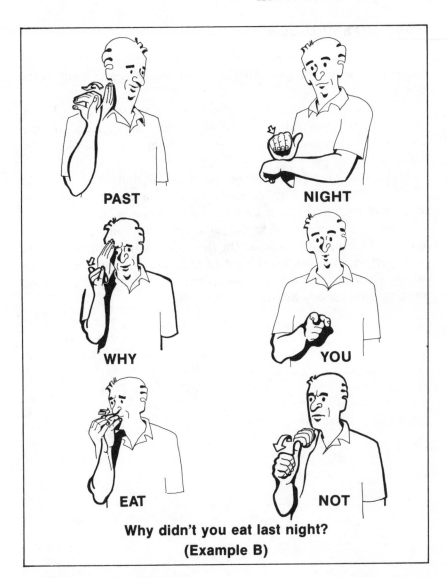

PAST

NIGHT

WHY

YOU

EAT

NOT

Why didn't you eat last night?
(Example B)

FACIAL EXPRESSIONS

We have given our cartoon character various facial expressions to emphasize the importance of facial expressions in ASL. The expressions are by no means the same all the time. The same sign will require different expressions at different times, depending upon the feeling you wish to convey.

SOME DO'S AND DON'TS

Try to avoid any bright light shining directly into the face of the person watching you. Bright lights are to deaf people what noise is to hearing people.

To get a deaf person's attention, stamp on the floor (if it is wooden), tap the table, or gently touch the person on the shoulder. If they are at a distance, wave your arm or blink a light off and on.

Make sure you do not stand or sit in the middle of someone else's conversation. This often happens in a crowded room or when two deaf people are seated far apart from each other.

Avoid such nervous behavior as drumming your fingers on a table or tapping your shoe on the floor. If you do such things, the deaf person will constantly turn to look at you to see what you want. Deaf people are extra-sensitive to vibrations, so avoid making unnecessary ones.

2

A Guide to Ameslan

In the United States there are several sign systems that should not be confused with Ameslan (ASL). These systems are ways of putting the English language into a manual-visual form; thus, they are called systems of Manually Coded English (MCEs). They are designed primarily for the purpose of teaching English to deaf children. An MCE uses the same signs that are used in ASL plus many new signs that have been created to serve special functions that do not exist in ASL. In an MCE the signs are arranged in accordance with the rules of English grammar. ASL, on the other hand, is not a way of coding English, but rather a language in and of itself. It differs from English in many respects. This book is concerned solely with ASL.

LIGHT, SIGHT, AND SPACE

Most languages are based entirely on sounds, and herein lies the unique difference between spoken language and ASL. Instead of sound waves in the form of spoken words, ASL uses light waves in the form of signs. ASL is a visual-spatial language. One *sees* ASL, and hearing plays absolutely no part in it. Because of this, ASL consists not only of signs made with the hands, but also of facial expressions, head movements, body movements, and an efficient use of the space around the signer. (In ASL the person "speaking" is the *signer,* and the person "listening" is the *watcher, observer,* or *reader.*) ASL is not mime, although mime sometimes is incorporated into the language.

The Sight Line

We begin the study of ASL with an understanding of how space is used. Imagine a line extending from the center of the signer's chest, straight out, parallel to the floor. This imaginary line is called the sight line. The sight line divides all space into the right or left side.

The Sight Line

Whenever the signer turns the body, the sight line moves with it.

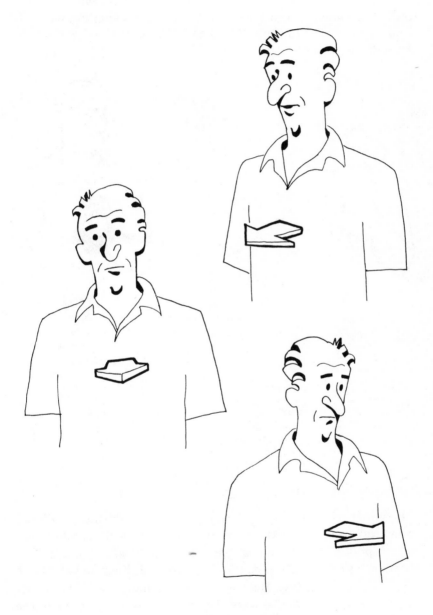

The Sight Line (3 views)

One of the most frequently used signs is a simple point with the index finger. When the signer points parallel to the sight line toward the watcher, it means "you." When the signer points to his or her own chest, it means "I" or "me." When the signer points to the right or the left of the sight line it means "he," "she," or "it."

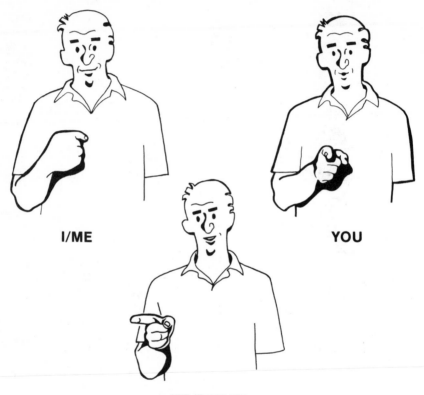

I/ME

YOU

HE/SHE/IT

Placement of Signs

People, places, objects, and events may be established or placed to the right and left of the sight line. Once this is done, the signer merely points to that space when reference to it is made. For example, as on page 21, suppose the signer tells the watcher, "I saw your father yesterday. He was driving a new car." The signer makes the sign for "see" toward the right.* This movement tells the

---

*Or toward the left, if the signer is left-handed.

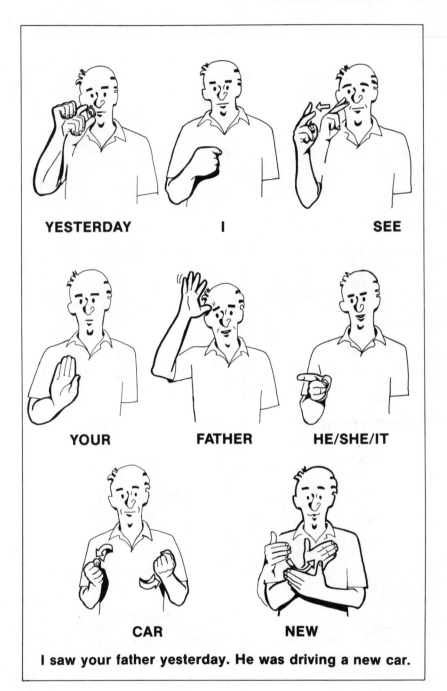

YESTERDAY   I   SEE

YOUR   FATHER   HE/SHE/IT

CAR   NEW

I saw your father yesterday. He was driving a new car.

YESTERDAY   I   GO TO

RESTAURANT   GO TO   MOVIE

GO TO   MUSEUM

Yesterday, I went to a restaurant,
a movie, and a museum.

watcher that the signer is about to say something about someone. Then the signer signs "father," and that tells the watcher who the someone is. The watcher also now knows that "father" occupies that space to the right of the sight line because the SEE sign moved toward that space. The signer my now point right, and it means "he," and it will continue to mean "he" (father) until the signer places someone or something else in that space.

Placement of more than one person, place, or object in the same space at the same time may not be done, but placement in other spaces at the same time may be done. For example, as on page 22, the signer may say, "Yesterday I went to a restaurant, a movie, and a museum." The three places are set up in three different spaces. Notice that the restaurant is nearer the signer, and the movie is farther out. Both may be to the right of the sight line, but they occupy slightly different spaces.

Avoid placing persons on the sight line itself. This space, with some exceptions, is reserved for the watcher. Any signs that move on or along the sight line have to do with the watcher, and no one else may occupy this area. An exception to this rule is illustrated by the following example:

| BOOK | HAVE | HE/SHE/IT | LIKE |

I have a book. It is interesting.

The signer first establishes the book, then points to it. When placing things on the sight line that have no reference to the watcher, place them near the signer and be sure to point to that space.

FACIAL EXPRESSIONS

In a spoken language, the rise and fall of the voice adds meaning to the words spoken. The various ways one can say "I love you" illustrate the importance of vocal inflection. The characteristic rising of the voice toward the end of a question is another example. In ASL, the face has these duties and supplies additional subtleties and nuances of meaning. Signs have meanings in and of themselves, just as words do, but these meanings are altered, shaped, enriched, and amplified by facial expressions. A face that is devoid of expression is to a deaf person the equivalent of a monotone speaker—boring and difficult to follow.

Facial expressions in ASL are especially important when asking questions. In general, when one asks a "wh" question (who, what, where, why, when, which, and how) the eyebrows usually go downward.

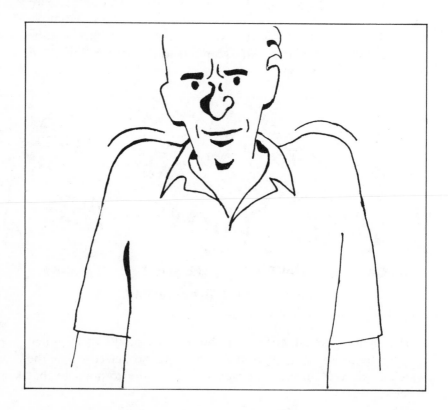

All other questions usually cause the eyebrows to move upward.

These are not rigid rules, and you may sometimes see something different, but these rules do generally apply. That the eyebrows will move up or down, however, is a certainty when asking questions.

The signer must learn to be expressive with the eyes and mouth as well as with the eyebrows. The eyes will open wide, or squint to narrow slits; the mouth will open and close; the lips will purse and stretch; the cheeks will puff out; and even the tongue will sometimes protrude.

BODY LANGUAGE

Body language is an essential element of ASL. Information is communicated not only by the face but also by the head, shoulders, torso, legs, and feet. The head may tilt forward, back, or to the side, especially when questions are asked.

The shoulders may shrug, the body may bend forward and backward and twist.

The incorporation of the whole body into the expression of sign language is absolutely required for clear, understandable communication. It is possible, of course, to overdo the matter, but it is better to err on the side of doing too much than too little. Deaf people are often described as animated, alive, vibrant, etc. This is due to their mastery of body language. For successful communication, you must do likewise.

PAST, PRESENT, FUTURE

One of the most difficult tasks in learning a new language is conjugating verbs in their various tenses. The struggle with regular and irregular verbs tries the student's patience to the utmost. It is, therefore, a pleasure to inform you that such is not the case with ASL. Learning to place actions in the past or future is comparatively simple.

No tenses are incorporated in the signs themselves. Tense is conveyed by using signs that tell when an action takes place, and these particular signs are called *time indicators*. In English for example, one may say, "I saw you." In ASL, the sign SEE is always made the same way whether it means "see," "sees," "seeing," "saw," or "seen:"

SEE

In order to sign the equivalent of "I saw you," it is necessary to use a time indicator. One may use signs that will place the event in a specific time, such as "yesterday," "last night," or "this morning."

YESTERDAY   **I**   **SEE**

Yesterday, I saw.

PAST   NIGHT   I   SEE

Last night, I saw.

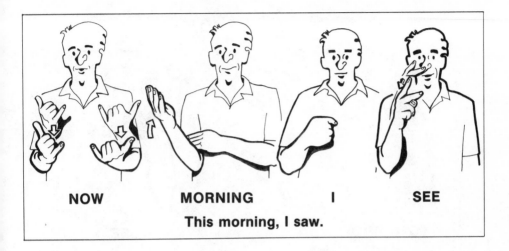

NOW   **MORNING**   **I**   **SEE**

This morning, I saw.

One may also use the FINISH sign to indicate no specific time, simply the past:

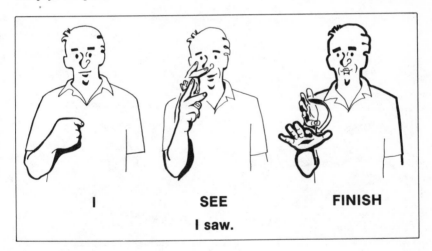

I   **SEE**   **FINISH**

I saw.

The use of a time indicator also applies to the future tense.

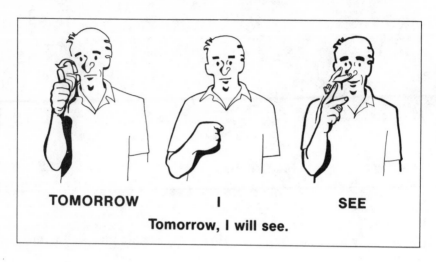

TOMORROW   **I**   **SEE**

Tomorrow, I will see.

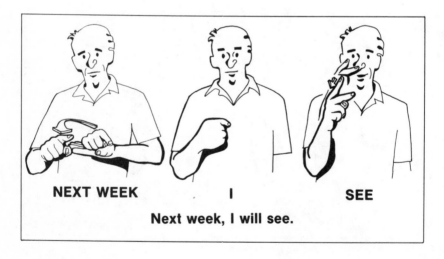

NEXT WEEK   **I**   **SEE**

Next week, I will see.

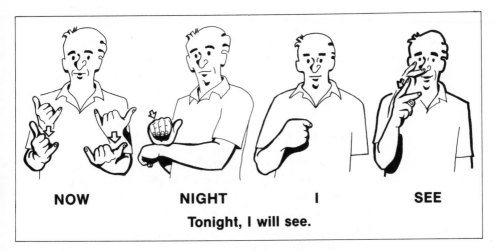

NOW   **NIGHT**   **I**   **SEE**

Tonight, I will see.

These phrases illustrate placing the event in a specific future time. For a nonspecific future time, use the WILL sign.

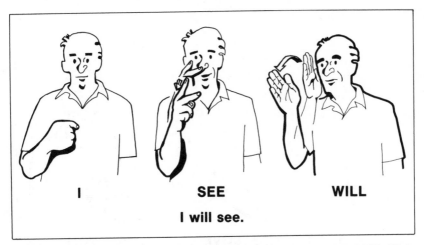

I   **SEE**   **WILL**

I will see.

Notice that both FINISH and WILL follow the verb SEE. This is generally true of nonspecific time indicators, whereas specific time indicators come at the beginning of a statement.

Context is used a great deal in ASL when establishing or determining tense. For instance, the signer may tell the watcher about an incident that occurred some time in the past or that will occur in the future. The signer will first establish the time of the incident by using a time indicator sign, then the signer will never repeat the time indicator sign or use any additional ones. The watcher knows that all the events described by the signer occur in the time frame established at the beginning of the statement by the time indicator sign used.

VERB DIRECTIONALITY

Verbs in ASL fall into three categories: non-directional verbs, one-directional verbs, and multi-directional verbs. Movement in verb signs may express who is performing an action (the subject) and to whom the action is directed (the indirect object). This quality of movement is called verb directionality.

The non-directional verbs do not express either subject or indirect object; therefore, these two things (subject and indirect object nouns and pronouns) must be supplied.

| I | LOVE | YOU |

I love you.

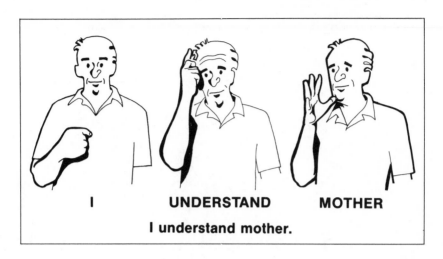

I   UNDERSTAND   MOTHER

I understand mother.

HE/SHE/IT   WANT   CAR

She wants a car.

The verbs LOVE, UNDERSTAND, and WANT in the sentences above do obviously have movement in them, but that movement does not express either subject or indirect object; that is, the movement has no directionality. Subject and indirect object signs must be supplied.

One-directional verb signs express indirect but not subject, as in these sentences:

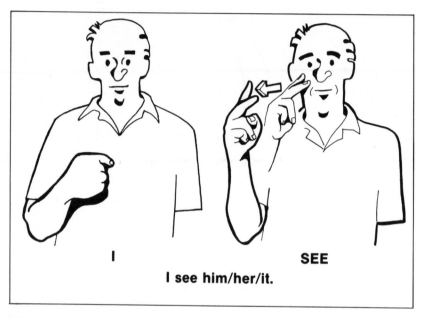

I   **SEE**

I see him/her/it.

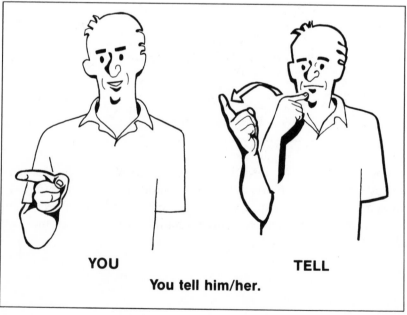

YOU   **TELL**

You tell him/her.

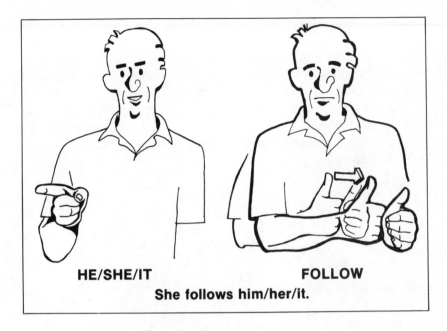

HE/SHE/IT **FOLLOW**
She follows him/her/it.

One-directional verbs move toward the indirect object; thus, a noun or pronoun is not required. The exception to this rule occurs when the signer is the indirect object. For example, "You see me" must be signed:

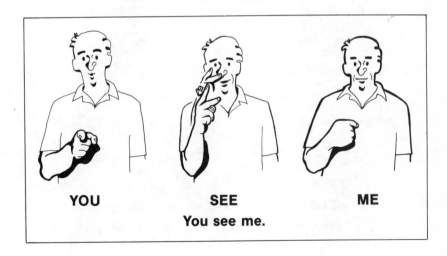

YOU **SEE** **ME**
You see me.

The indirect object here is the signer ("me"), and since the movement of the SEE sign does not move toward the indirect object, then the indirect object must be signed. Notice also that the SEE sign does indeed move slightly to the right of the sight line, not directly toward the watcher.

The movement of multi-directional signs expresses both subject and indirect object. The sign moves from the subject toward the indirect object; thus, neither the subject nor indirect object is signed. Examples:

HELP
I help you.*

HELP
He helps me.

HELP
He helps her.

---

*In this illustration, the body is faced to your left to give you a better view of how the sign is made, but the sign itself goes along the sight line from the signer to the watcher.

The movement from a space normally implies that whoever occupies that space is the subject. The movement toward a space normally implies that whoever occupies that space is the indirect object.

TO BE OR NOT TO BE

Many sentences in English require some form of the "to be" verb. Examples of such sentences include "I am fine," "You are tired," "Where is Joe?," and "They were not here." There is no "to be" verb in ASL. The above examples are signed, "I FINE," "YOU TIRED," "WHERE JOE?," and "THEY NOT HERE." Statements such as "It is raining," "The flower is growing," and "The train is late" are signed:

RAIN

It is raining.

FLOWER   **GROW**

The flower is growing.

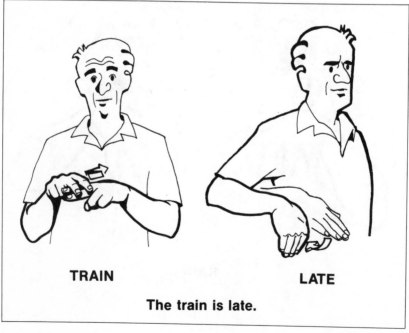

TRAIN   **LATE**

The train is late.

When the signer wishes to stress or emphasize statements, then the TRUE sign is used. The following statement means simply that I am sick:

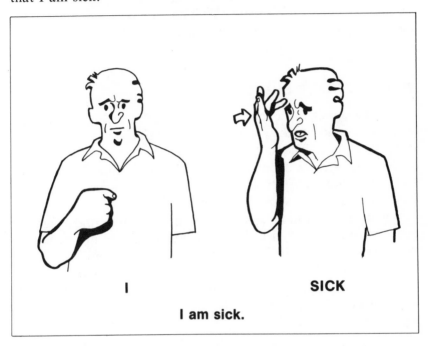

I	SICK

I am sick.

The following statement means that I am really sick, or I am very sick:

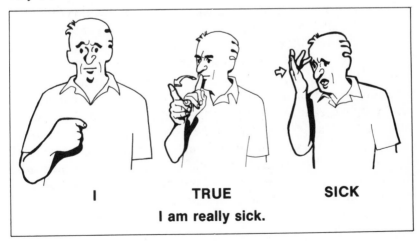

I	TRUE	SICK

I am really sick.

Do not confuse the use of the TRUE sign as a sign of stress and emphasis with a form of the "to be" verb in English.

The TRUE sign also means true, truly, real, really, sure, surely, certainly, indeed, and actually. When used alone with a questioning expression, the TRUE sign means "Is that so?" or "Are you sure?"

WORDS VERSUS SIGNS

A word stands for a concept or an idea. If someone says "tree," you understand immediately because you have in your mind the concept of tree. The same applies to signs. If the signer signs TREE, the watcher understands it immediately without having to think the word "tree". In other words, a sign stands for an idea or concept; it does not stand for a word.

When you form statements in ASL, do not try to find a sign for every word in the English statement. Languages do not work that way. (For example, in English one says, "I am hungry," but in Spanish and French one says, "I have hunger." In ASL one says, "I hunger.") First get clearly in mind the ideas you want to communicate, forget the words, and then find the appropriate signs to express the ideas.

SIGN ORDER

The order of words in a language is called the syntax. In ASL we talk of sign-order rather than word-order. The syntax of ASL is sometimes very flexible, permitting any one of several arrangements of signs, while at other times the syntax is rigidly fixed.

One guide to ASL syntax is that the signs are arranged in the same order in which the events they represent occurred in real life. A simple example of this is the sentence, "I am going home after work." The arrangement of the words here is not in the same order in which these events can occur. One cannot go home until work is over. ASL arranges the signs so that the statement reads, "After work I am going home." You must develop the habit of thinking: What comes first, then second, then next?

In the statement, "I am worried about Walter, who was in an

accident last week," the events are related out of sequence and the specific time indicator comes at the end of the sentence. ASL first sets up the time (last week) with the specific time indicator, then tells that Walter was in an accident, and finally gives the response to it. The sentence then reads, "Last week, Walter was in an accident and I am worried." This example also contains another guide to ASL syntax, the cause-and-effect relationship of events. I could not be worried about Walter before his accident; my worrying is the effect caused by the accident. So it must come in the sentence after the accident.

Another example of this cause-and-effect relationship can be seen in this sentence: "I get nervous when a black cat crosses my path." The nervousness is the effect of seeing a black cat cross my path, so the sentence in ASL reads, "When a black cat crosses my path, I get nervous." Always arrange the signs so that the cause comes before the effect.

It is often useful to think in cinematic terms. When you wish to relate a story, think of it as a movie filmed in continuous time with no flashbacks or flash-forwards. Each scene leads chronologically into the next scene. (The camera would show the black cat walking across your path, for example, then show your reaction to it. If the camera shows your reaction first, then shows the black cat crossing your path, the camera is flashing backwards in time.) Arrange the events, persons, and details in this manner and you will be following good ASL syntax. Two more syntactic features are described in the next two sections.

HOW TO SAY NO

The most common way to negate a statement in ASL is to shake the head while you are making a sign. For example, to say "I do not understand," shake your head as you sign "I understand." The shaking of the head negates the statement so that it means "I do not understand." This practice applies to nearly all signs, including negative signs themselves. If the signer adds NOT in the above statement, and simultaneously shakes the head, the negation is emphasized. We know that English grammar does not permit double negatives, but in Spanish one may say "Yo no sé nada," which literally means "I not know nothing." Spanish here may be compared to ASL, where one may sign UNDERSTAND NOTHING while shaking the head, thus creating a double negative.

Signs of negation usually follow the thing they negate, as in the following sentences:

I   TELL   NOT

I'm not telling.

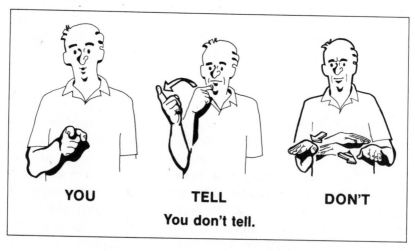

YOU   TELL   DON'T

You don't tell.

HE/SHE/IT   **TELL ME**   **NONE**

It tells me nothing.

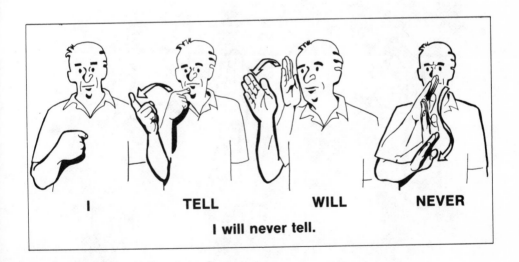

I   **TELL**   **WILL**   **NEVER**

I will never tell.

Many signs have negation build into them:

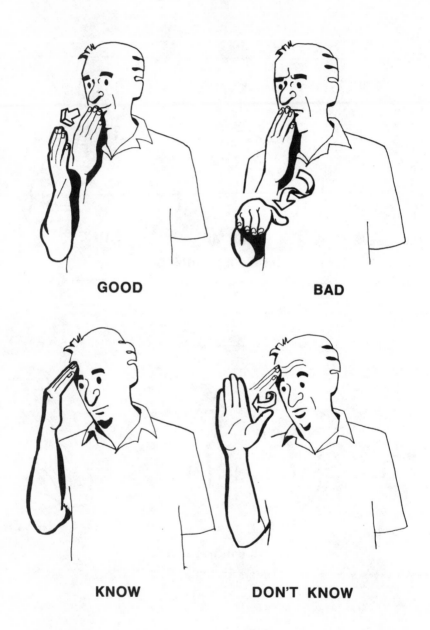

GOOD   BAD

KNOW   DON'T KNOW

LIKE

DON'T LIKE

WANT

DON'T WANT

The signer should always shake the head while simultaneously making the negative form of the sign.

INTERROGATIVES

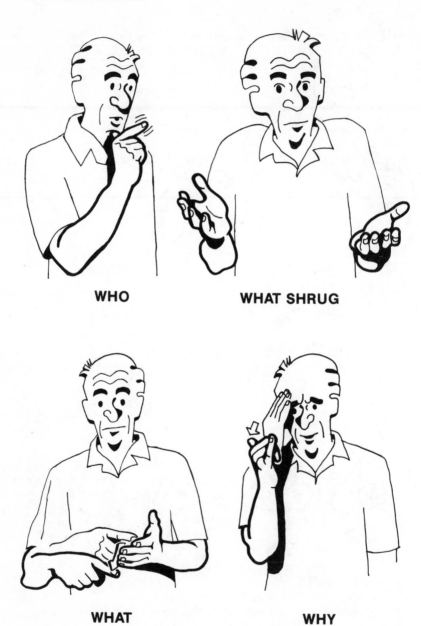

WHO   WHAT SHRUG

WHAT   WHY

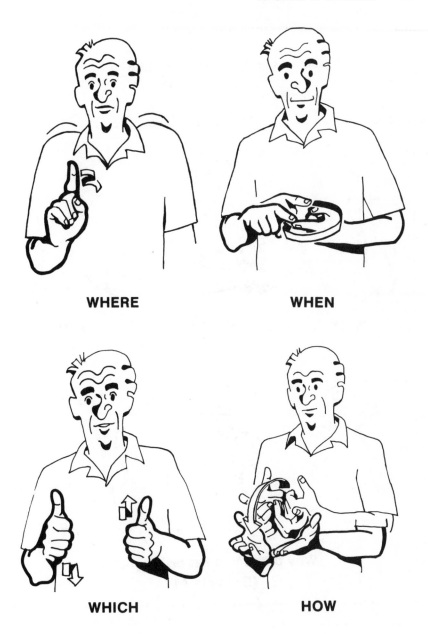

WHERE   **WHEN**

WHICH   **HOW**

In ASL, the signs WHO, WHAT, WHY, WHERE, WHEN, WHICH, and HOW generally come at the end of a question, but may also be at the beginning of a question. Sometimes you will even see them at the beginning and the end of a question. Examples of sentences using interrogatives include:

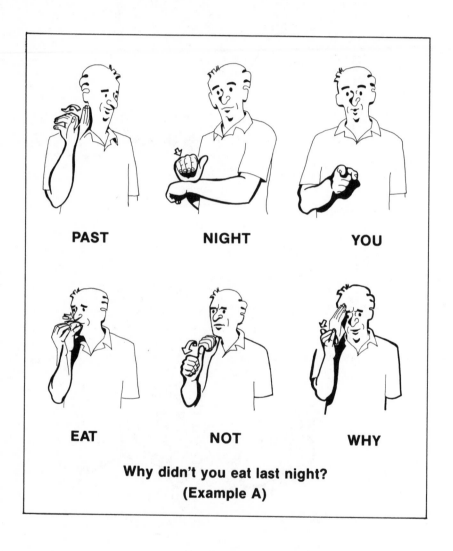

Why didn't you eat last night?
(Example A)

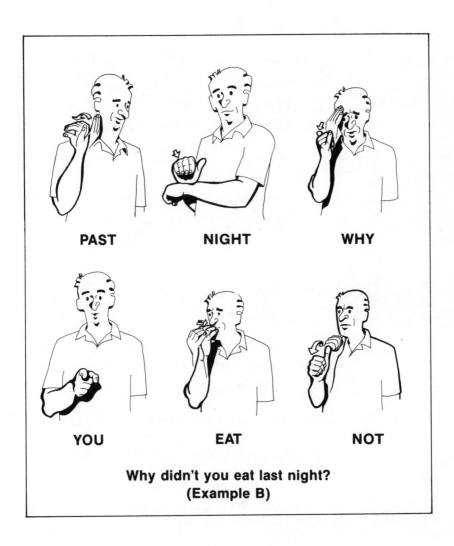

PAST　　　　**NIGHT**　　　　**WHY**

YOU　　　　**EAT**　　　　**NOT**

Why didn't you eat last night?
(Example B)

COFFEE   **TEA**   **WANT**   **WHICH**

Which do you want, coffee or tea?

(Example A)

WANT   **WHICH**   **COFFEE**   **TEA**

Which do you want, coffee or tea?

(Example B)

Naturally the signer makes a questioning facial expression when using these interrogatives.

PLURALS

Often signs are repeated or moved in such a way that shows plurality. Some plurals are shown at the top of page 53:

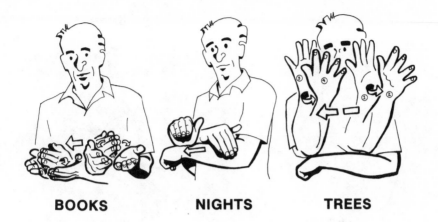

BOOKS   **NIGHTS**   **TREES**

When a sign does not lend itself to this kind of repetition or pluralizing movement, then signers use such signs as MANY, FEW, and SOME, or they use specific numbers such as NINE or FIFTY.

PRONOUNS

All the pronouns may be expressed by just three hand shapes. The first group is made up of the pointing pronouns. Simply point to get: I, me, you, he, she, him, her, it.

The second group is the posessive pronouns:

MY   **HIS/HER/ITS**

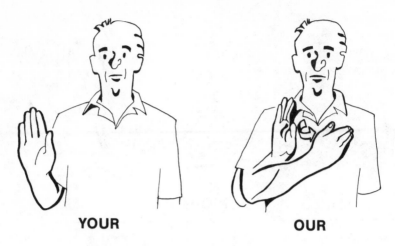

YOUR   **OUR**

The third group is the self pronouns:

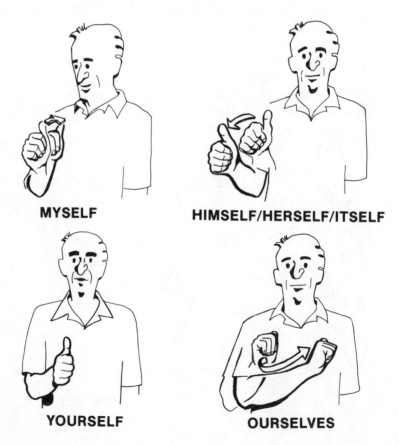

MYSELF   **HIMSELF/HERSELF/ITSELF**

YOURSELF   **OURSELVES**

Third person plural pronouns move in a very small arc:

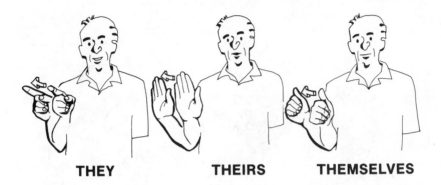

THEY   **THEIRS**   **THEMSELVES**

First and second person singular pointing pronouns tend to come at the end of a statement:

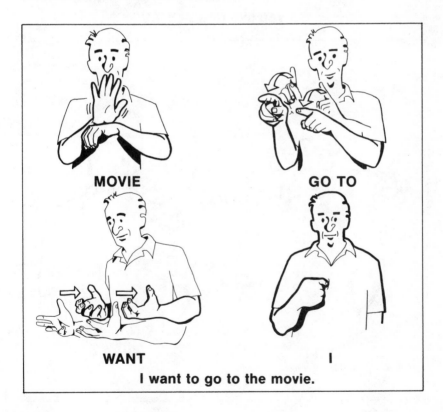

MOVIE   **GO TO**

WANT   **I**

I want to go to the movie.

Sometimes the first and second person singular point pronoun is dropped entirely, especially in questions:

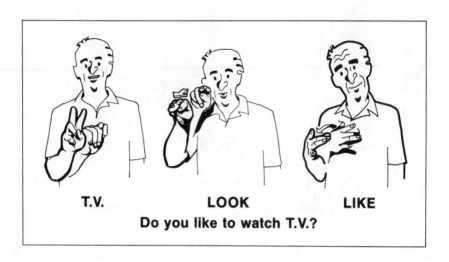

T.V.   **LOOK**   **LIKE**

Do you like to watch T.V.?

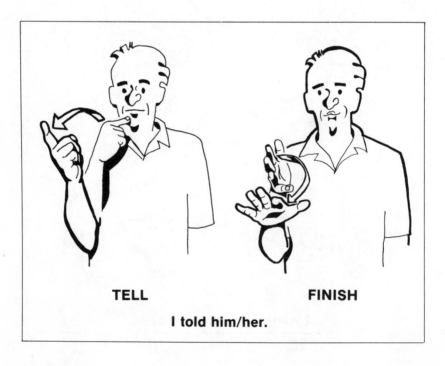

TELL   **FINISH**

I told him/her.

The second statement on page 56 is a simple declarative statement of fact, so you may assume the subject is "I." If the intent were "You told him," then the sentence would be:

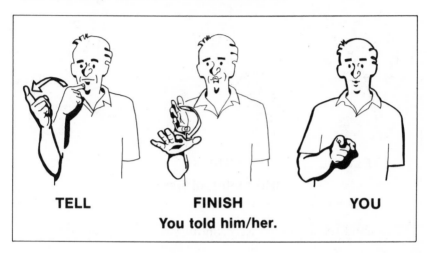

TELL   **FINISH**   **YOU**

You told him/her.

The second person singular pointing pronoun is usually dropped in questions, as below:

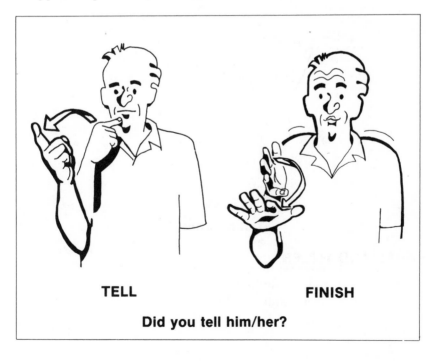

TELL   **FINISH**

Did you tell him/her?

If the intent here were "Did I tell him?," then it would be signed:

TELL   **FINISH**   **I**

Did I tell him/her?

Command forms rarely use pronouns:

TELL

Tell him/her!

NAMES AND TITLES

When deaf people are talking to each other they rarely use each other's names. For example, "How are you, Bob?" becomes simply, "How you?" If, however, the signer asks the watcher about another person, then the signer uses that person's name. ("How is Bob?")

A person's name must be fingerspelled, but most deaf people also have name-signs. A name-sign is one that stands for that person, not for the name. Two people with the same name will have different name-signs. When you first meet a deaf person, you fingerspell your name. You tell him your name-sign only if he asks. Usually name-signs are not asked for until the relationship develops beyond that of a casual acquaintance.

Titles such as "Mrs.," "Dr.," and "Rev." are fingerspelled and used only when the person is being introduced. You never use them when you are talking directly to the person. "How are you, Dr. Smith?" becomes simply "How you?"

ARTICLES

There are no articles (a, an, the) in ASL.

A FINAL WORD

The acquisition of a spoken language involves principally learning grammar, pronunciation, and vocabulary. Except for pronunciation, the same applies to learning ASL. Forming signs clearly is the equivalent of pronunciation in ASL. Clarity in signing depends upon accuracy in making the sign, smoothness in execution of the sign, flow from one sign to the next without jerky or hesitant movements, the use of facial expressions, the use of head and body movements, and the proper use of space. The only way to develop these is through using the language with deaf people. They will correct you when you err, and by watching them carefully you will correct and fine tune yourself.

3

Everyday Expressions

HELLO

Hello.

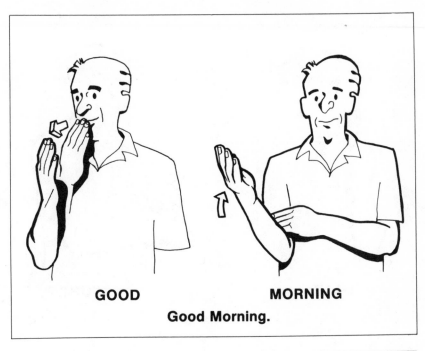

GOOD   **MORNING**

Good Morning.

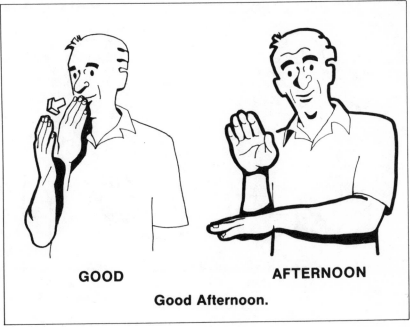

GOOD   **AFTERNOON**

Good Afternoon.

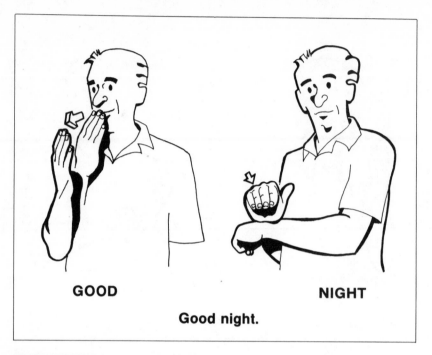

GOOD NIGHT

Good night.

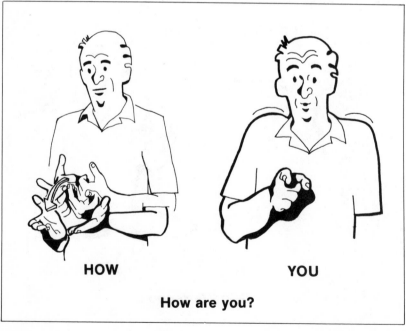

HOW YOU

How are you?

UP TILL NOW   **HOW**

How have you been?

HAPPY   **SEE**

I'm glad to see you.

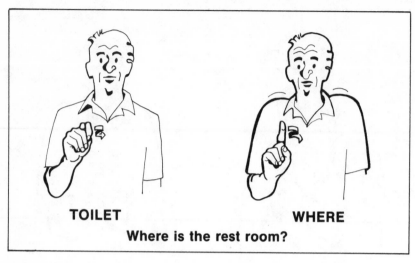

TOILET   **WHERE**

Where is the rest room?

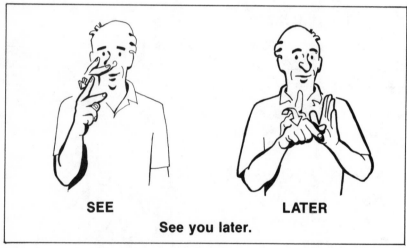

SEE   **LATER**

See you later.

GOOD-BYE

Good-Bye.

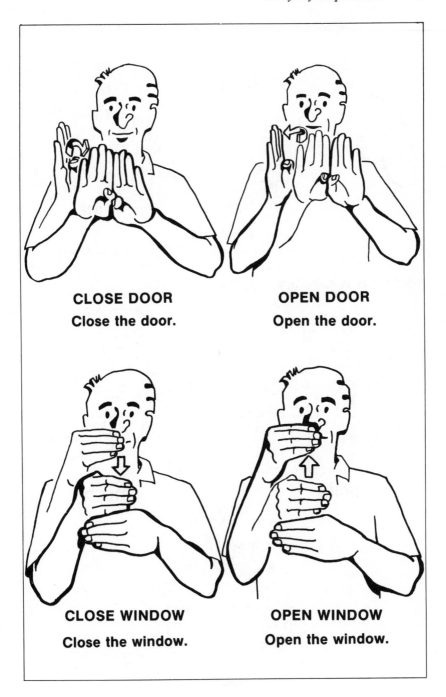

CLOSE DOOR
Close the door.

OPEN DOOR
Open the door.

CLOSE WINDOW
Close the window.

OPEN WINDOW
Open the window.

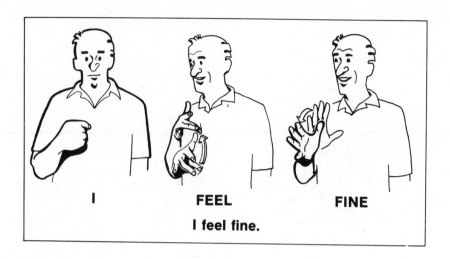

I　　FEEL　　FINE

I feel fine.

Additional vocabulary:

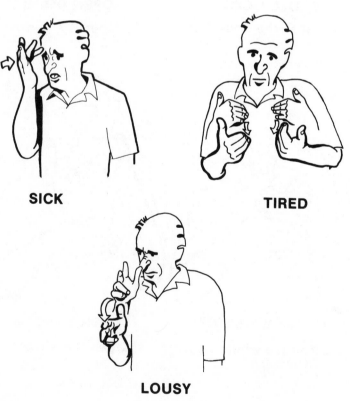

SICK

TIRED

LOUSY

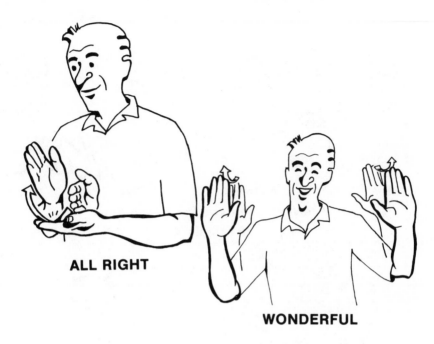

ALL RIGHT

WONDERFUL

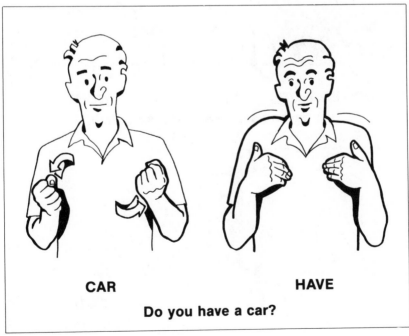

CAR

HAVE

Do you have a car?

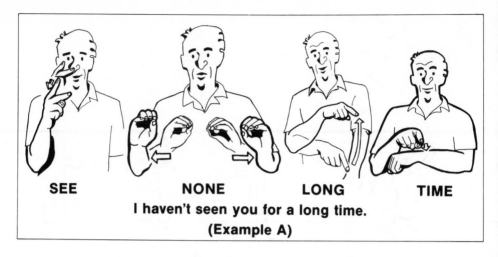

SEE   NONE   LONG   TIME

I haven't seen you for a long time.
(Example A)

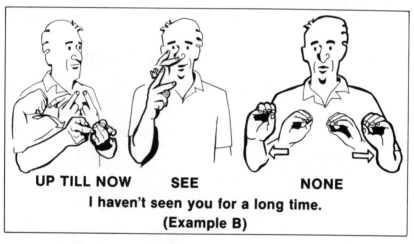

UP TILL NOW   SEE   NONE

I haven't seen you for a long time.
(Example B)

GOOD
Thank you.

PLEASE
Please.

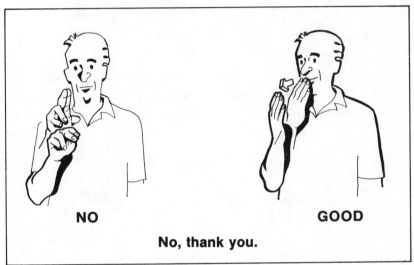

NO

GOOD

No, thank you.

EXCUSE
Pardon me.

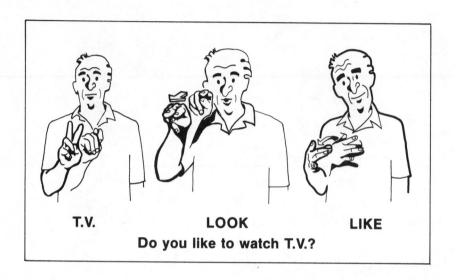

T.V.   **LOOK**   **LIKE**

Do you like to watch T.V.?

MOVIE   **GO TO**   **WANT**

Do you want to go to the movies?

PHONE   **NUMBER**   **WHAT SHRUG**

What's your phone number?

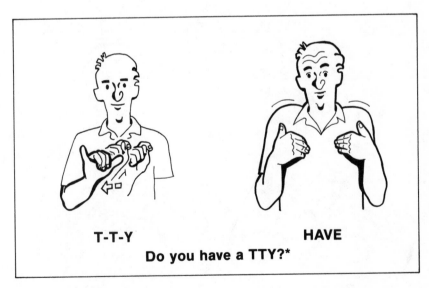

T-T-Y   **HAVE**

Do you have a TTY?*

*The TTY or TDD is a device that permits one to type messages back and forth over the telephone.

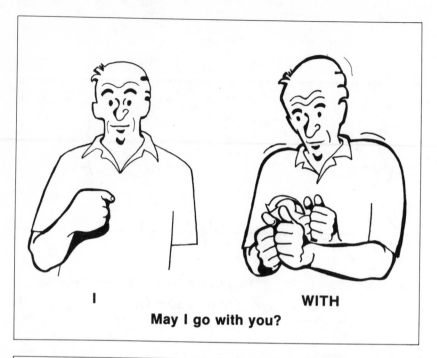

I   WITH

May I go with you?

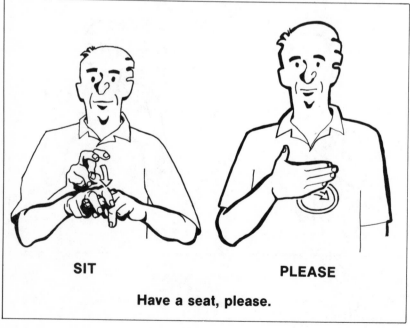

SIT   PLEASE

Have a seat, please.

TIME

What time is it?

HOME   **GO**   **MUST**

I have to go home.

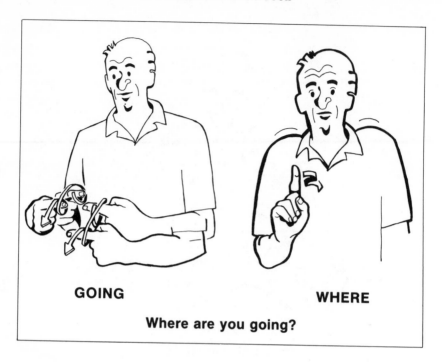

GOING　　　　　　**WHERE**

Where are you going?

SORRY

I'm sorry.

4

Signing and Deafness

I   LEARN   SIGN   LANGUAGE

I'm learning sign language.

The sign LANGUAGE is usually not signed in this expression, so that it reads literally: "I am learning to sign."

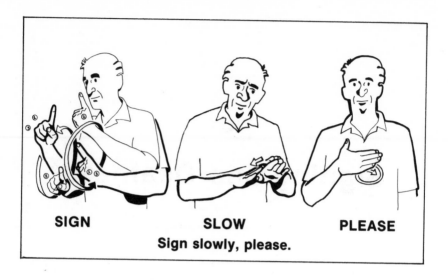

SIGN   **SLOW**   **PLEASE**

Sign slowly, please.

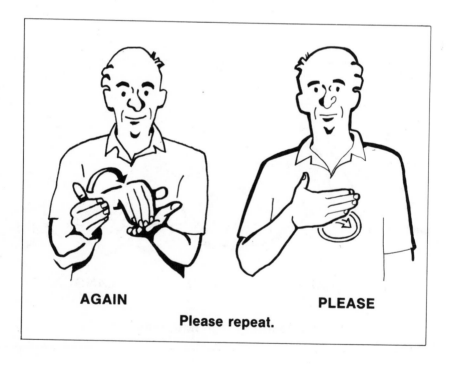

AGAIN   **PLEASE**

Please repeat.

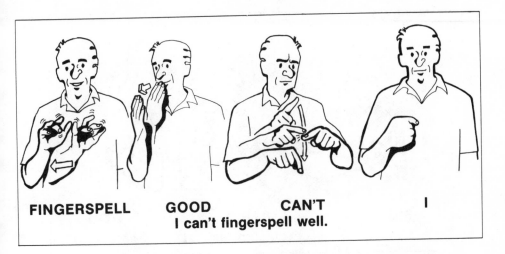

FINGERSPELL **GOOD** **CAN'T** **I**

I can't fingerspell well.

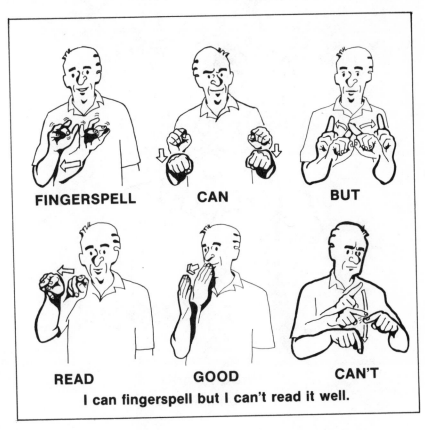

FINGERSPELL **CAN** **BUT**

READ **GOOD** **CAN'T**

I can fingerspell but I can't read it well.

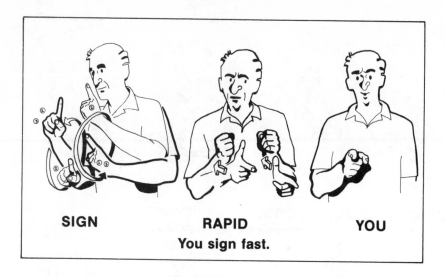

SIGN   **RAPID**   **YOU**

You sign fast.

UNDERSTAND

I don't understand.

WRITE   **PLEASE**

Would you write it, please?

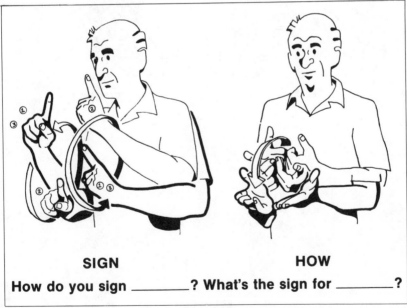

SIGN   **HOW**

How do you sign _____? What's the sign for _____?

Ask these questions by pointing to whatever it is you want to know the sign for or by fingerspelling the word.

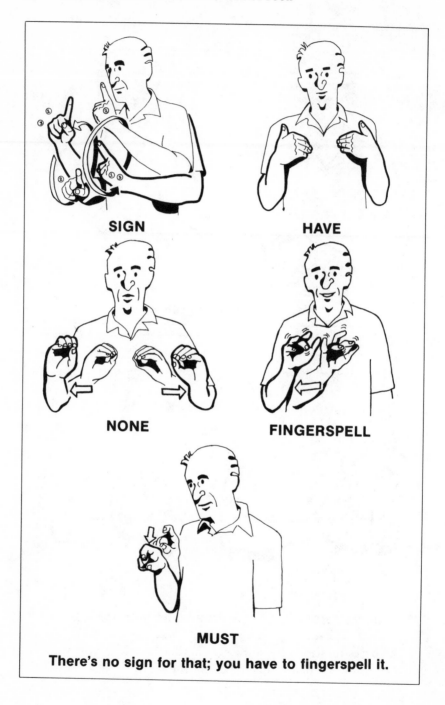

SIGN

HAVE

NONE

FINGERSPELL

MUST

There's no sign for that; you have to fingerspell it.

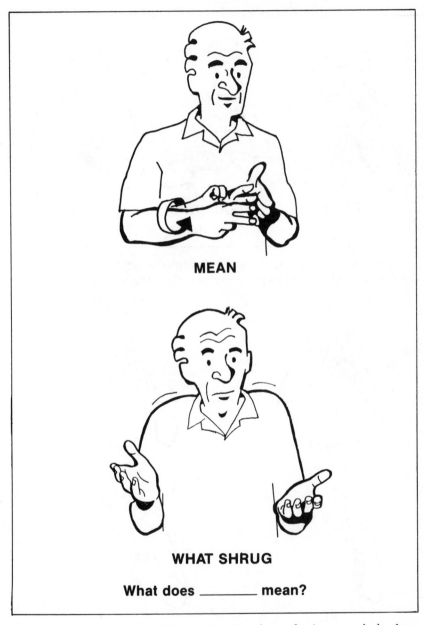

MEAN

WHAT SHRUG

What does _____ mean?

To ask this question, first make the sign of whatever it is that you want to know the meaning of, then sign MEAN WHAT SHRUG.

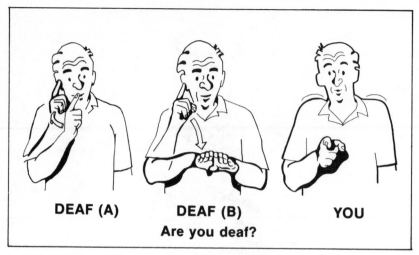

DEAF (A)   DEAF (B)   YOU
Are you deaf?

Either way of signing "deaf" is acceptable, but deaf people use the first one shown above more often than the second one.

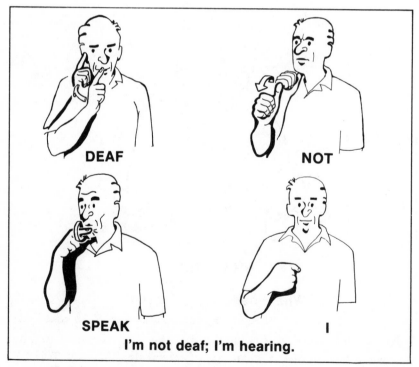

DEAF   NOT

SPEAK   I
I'm not deaf; I'm hearing.

Hearing people are referred to as "speaking" people.

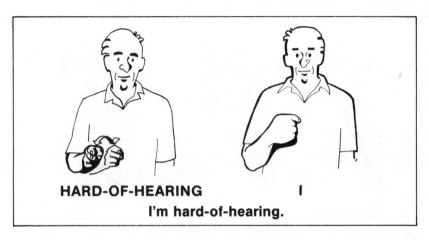

HARD-OF-HEARING   **I**

I'm hard-of-hearing.

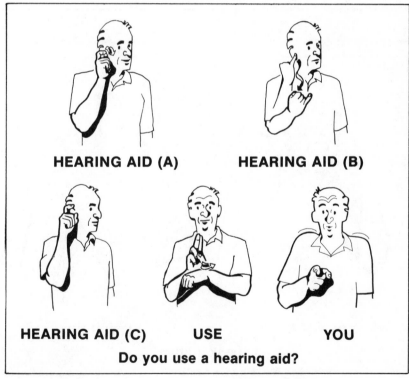

HEARING AID (A)   **HEARING AID (B)**

HEARING AID (C)   **USE**   **YOU**

Do you use a hearing aid?

The first two signs for "hearing aid" shown here represent the kind of aid that is attached by a cord to a unit worn on the body. The third kind is the type worn behind the ear.

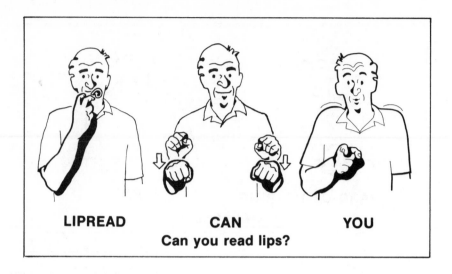

LIPREAD   **CAN**   **YOU**

Can you read lips?

SPEAK   **LITTLE BIT**

I speak a little.

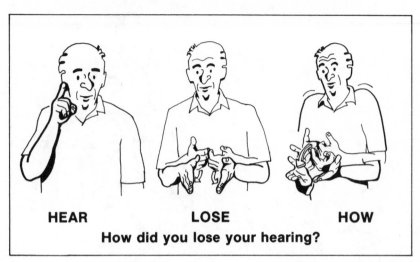

HEAR   **LOSE**   **HOW**

How did you lose your hearing?

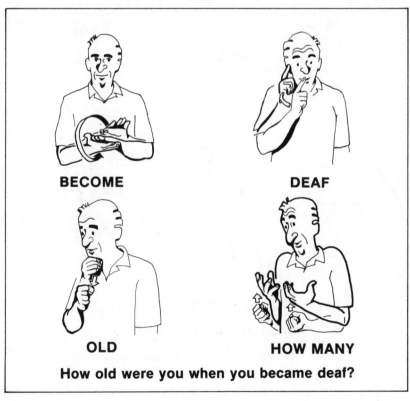

BECOME   **DEAF**

OLD   **HOW MANY**

How old were you when you became deaf?

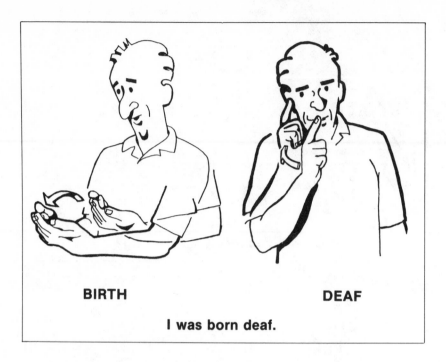

BIRTH   **DEAF**

I was born deaf.

FATHER   **MOTHER**   **DEAF**

Are your parents deaf?

C-L-U-B

VISIT   **WANT**   **I**

I want to visit the club for deaf people.

Fingerspell "C-L-U-B" at the beginning of this sentence. It is not necessary to sign "for deaf people", because the word "club" implies that.

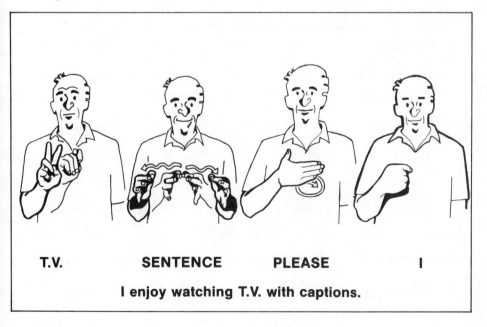

T.V.   **SENTENCE**   **PLEASE**   **I**

I enjoy watching T.V. with captions.

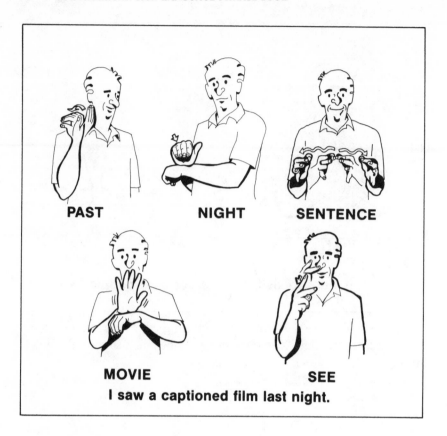

PAST   **NIGHT**   **SENTENCE**

MOVIE   **SEE**

I saw a captioned film last night.

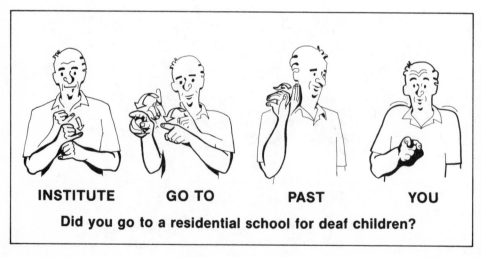

INSTITUTE   **GO TO**   **PAST**   **YOU**

Did you go to a residential school for deaf children?

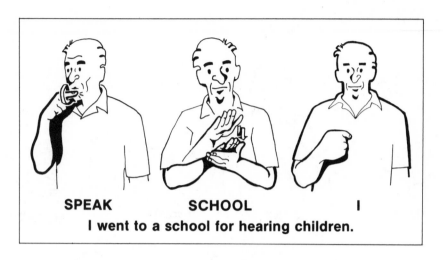

SPEAK   **SCHOOL**   **I**

I went to a school for hearing children.

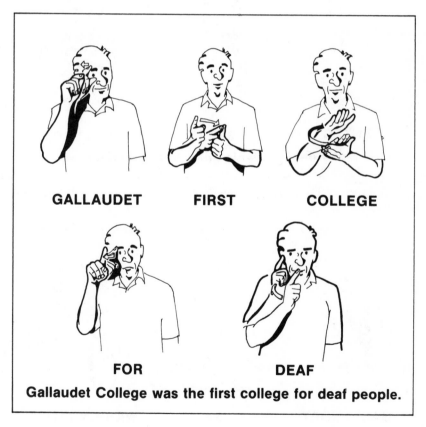

GALLAUDET   **FIRST**   **COLLEGE**

FOR   **DEAF**

Gallaudet College was the first college for deaf people.

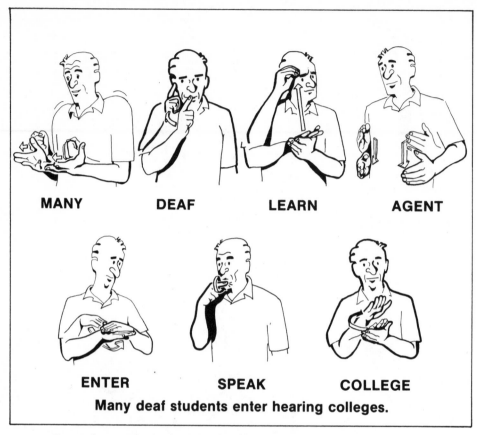

MANY   DEAF   LEARN   AGENT

ENTER   SPEAK   COLLEGE

Many deaf students enter hearing colleges.

Sometimes "D-C" is fingerspelled after the sign for "Washington."

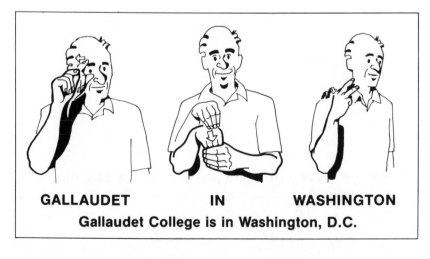

GALLAUDET   IN   WASHINGTON

Gallaudet College is in Washington, D.C.

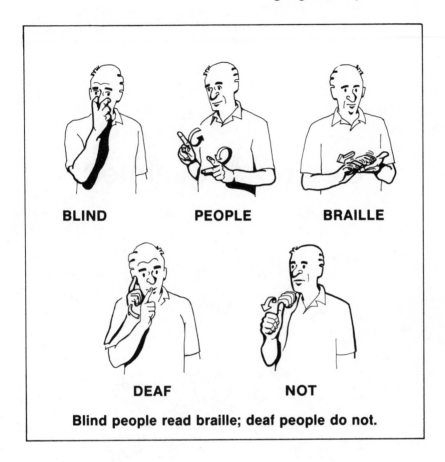

BLIND   **PEOPLE**   **BRAILLE**

DEAF   **NOT**

Blind people read braille; deaf people do not.

5
Getting Acquainted

NAME　　　　　　WHAT SHRUG

What is your name?

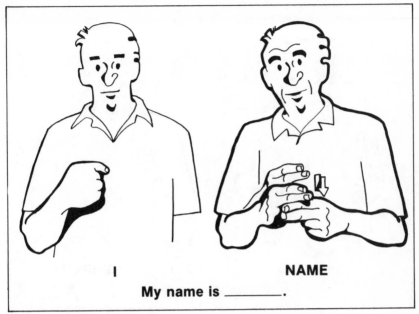

I

NAME

My name is _____.

Fingerspell your name.

HAPPY

MEET

I'm happy to meet you.

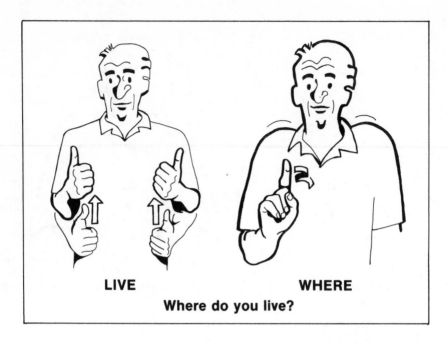

LIVE   **WHERE**

Where do you live?

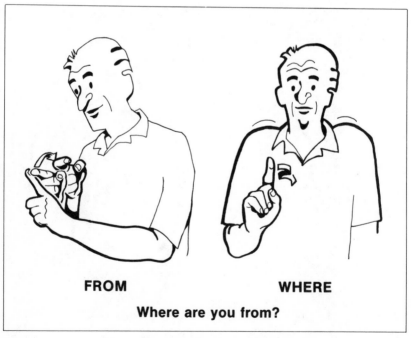

FROM   **WHERE**

Where are you from?

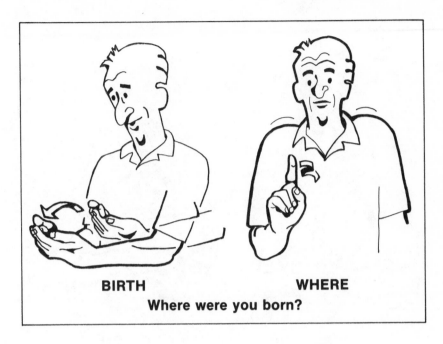

BIRTH   **WHERE**

Where were you born?

INTRODUCE   **WIFE**

May I introduce my wife?

After making the sign for the person you are introducing, you then fingerspell that person's name.

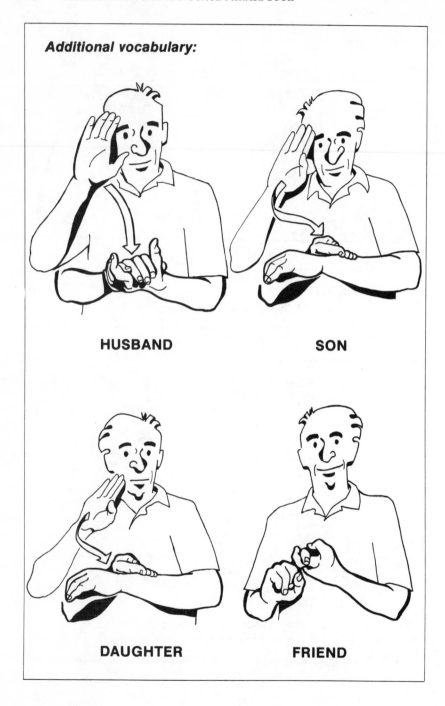

Additional vocabulary:

HUSBAND

SON

DAUGHTER

FRIEND

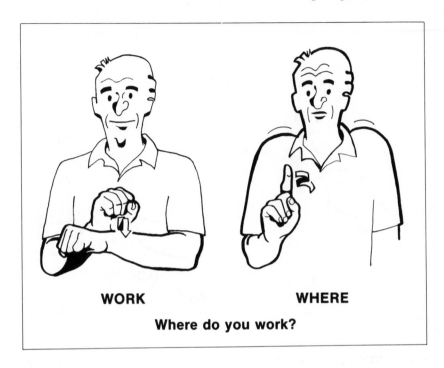

WORK   **WHERE**

Where do you work?

WORK   **MAJOR**   **WHAT SHRUG**

What kind of work do you do?

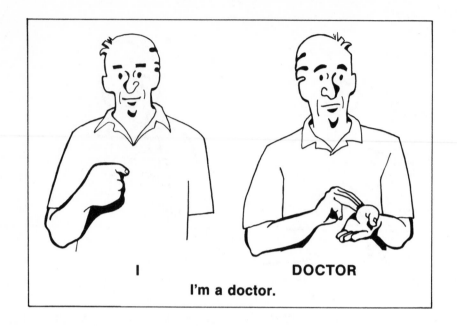

I   **DOCTOR**

I'm a doctor.

Additional vocabulary:

LAW   **TEACH**

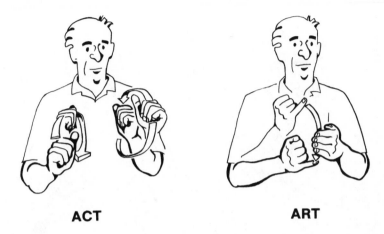

ACT   **ART**

The AGENT sign is often added to a verb or noun sign to indicate that one does or is what the verb or noun sign says. Here the AGENT sign could be added to TEACH, LAW, ACT, and ART, but would not be added to DOCTOR, POLICE, HOUSE-WIFE, FIREFIGHTER, or SECRETARY. The use of the AGENT sign is optional.

AGENT   **FIREFIGHTER**

POLICE   **SECRETARY**

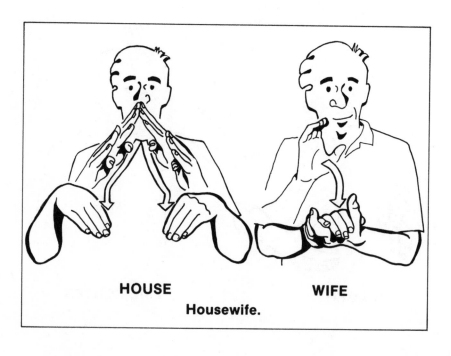

HOUSE   **WIFE**

Housewife.

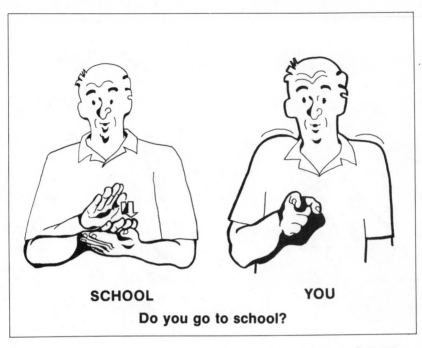

SCHOOL **YOU**

Do you go to school?

MARRY **YOU**

Are you married?

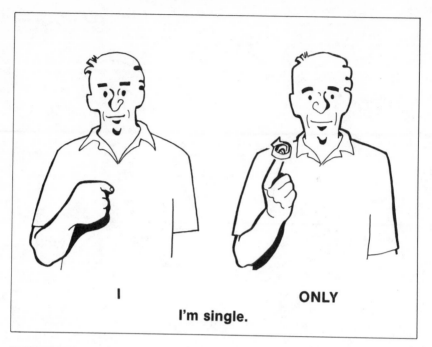

I   ONLY

I'm single.

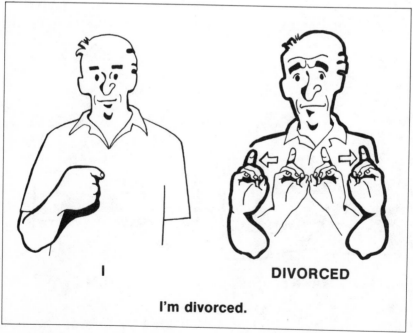

I   DIVORCED

I'm divorced.

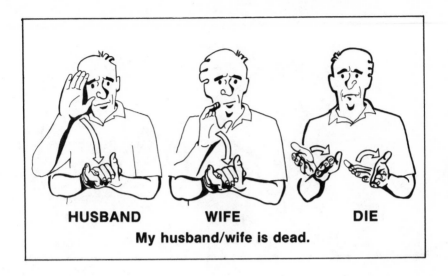

HUSBAND   **WIFE**   **DIE**

My husband/wife is dead.

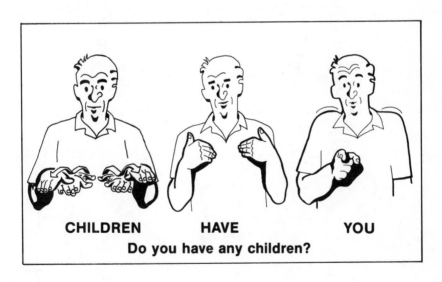

CHILDREN   **HAVE**   **YOU**

Do you have any children?

CHILDREN   **HAVE**   **HOW MANY**

How many children do you have?

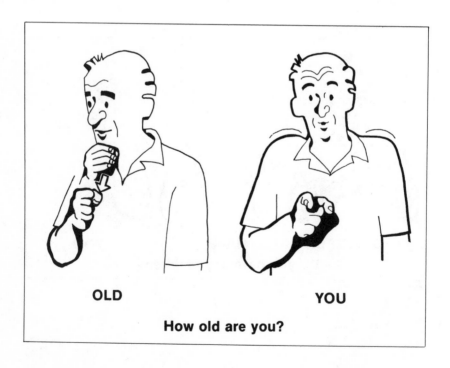

OLD   **YOU**

How old are you?

SMOKE CIGARETTE   **COMPLAIN**

Do you mind if I smoke?

ALL RIGHT
It's all right. It's okay.

SMOKE CIGARETTE   **PROHIBIT**

Smoking is not allowed.

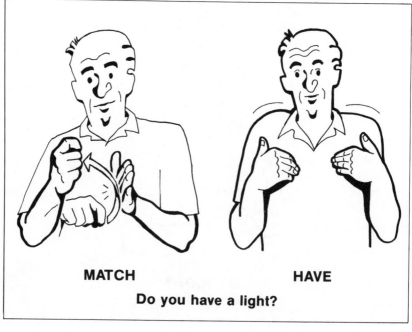

MATCH   **HAVE**

Do you have a light?

6

Health

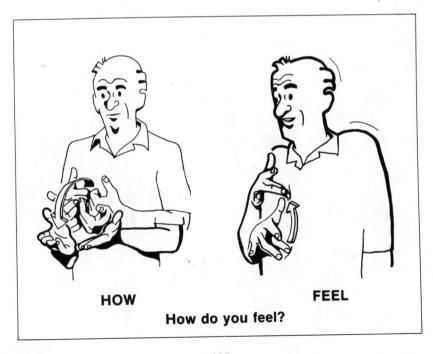

HOW   FEEL

How do you feel?

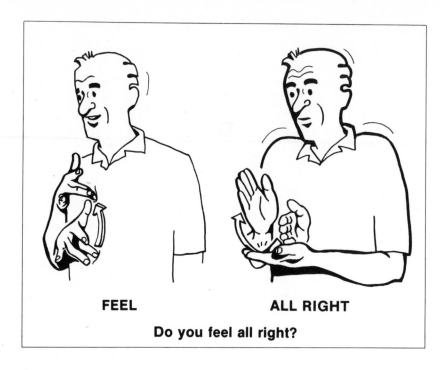

FEEL   **ALL RIGHT**

Do you feel all right?

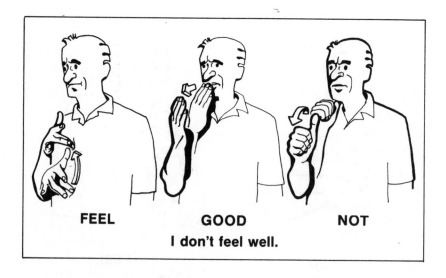

FEEL   **GOOD**   **NOT**

I don't feel well.

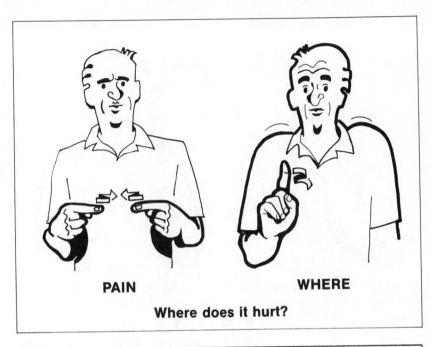

PAIN **WHERE**

Where does it hurt?

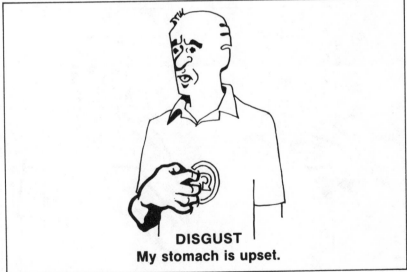

DISGUST
My stomach is upset.

When done alone, as it is done here, this sign may also mean that something is disgusting. Context determines which meaning is intended.

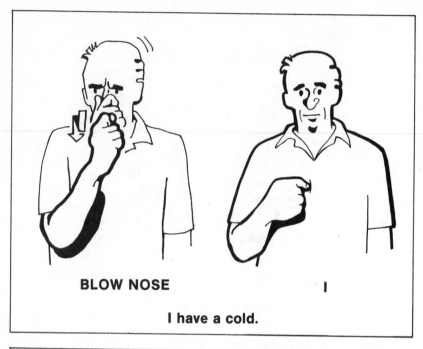

BLOW NOSE   I

I have a cold.

RUNNY NOSE   I

My nose is runny.

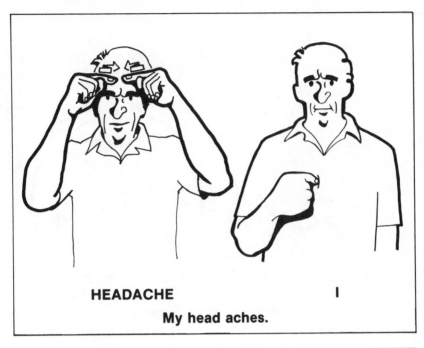

HEADACHE   **I**

My head aches.

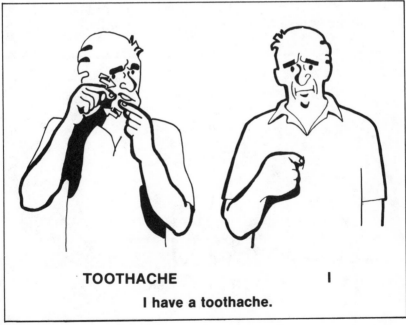

TOOTHACHE   **I**

I have a toothache.

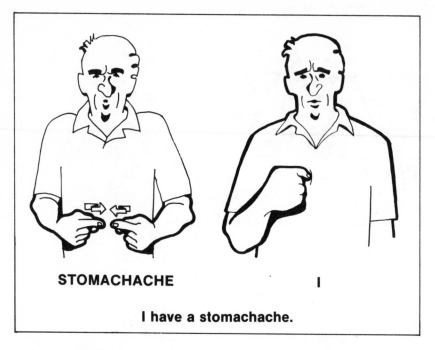

STOMACHACHE **I**

I have a stomachache.

The sign PAIN may be placed anywhere on the body to denote that you are hurt or have a pain in that part of the body.

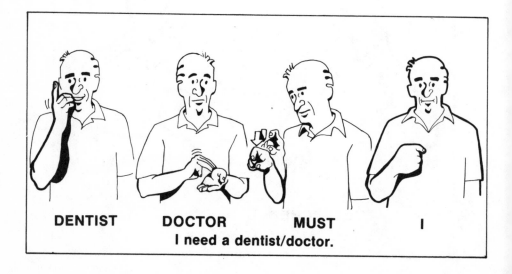

DENTIST **DOCTOR** **MUST** **I**

I need a dentist/doctor.

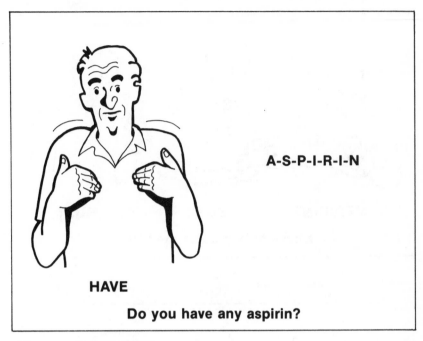

A-S-P-I-R-I-N

HAVE

Do you have any aspirin?

Fingerspell ASPIRIN.

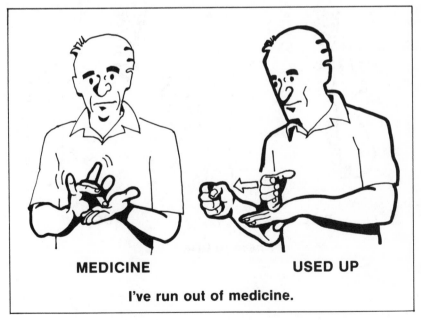

MEDICINE　　　　**USED UP**

I've run out of medicine.

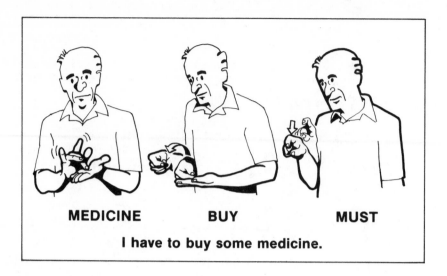

MEDICINE   BUY   MUST

I have to buy some medicine.

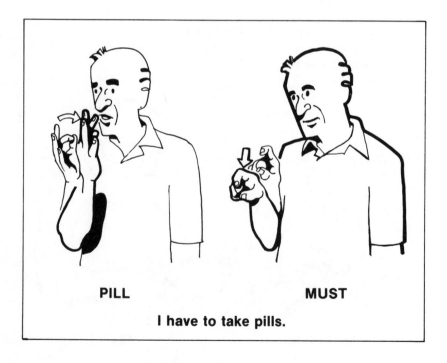

PILL   MUST

I have to take pills.

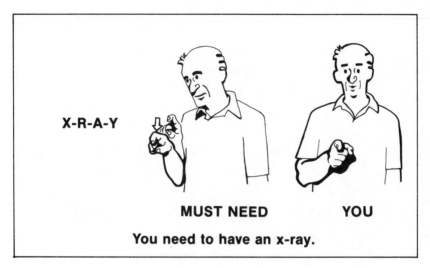

X-R-A-Y

MUST NEED   YOU

You need to have an x-ray.

Fingerspell X-RAY.

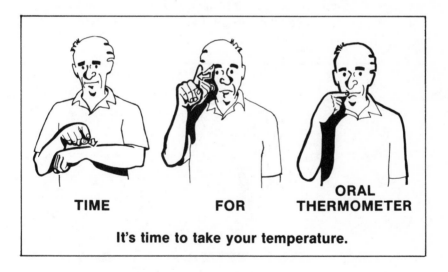

TIME   FOR   ORAL
THERMOMETER

It's time to take your temperature.

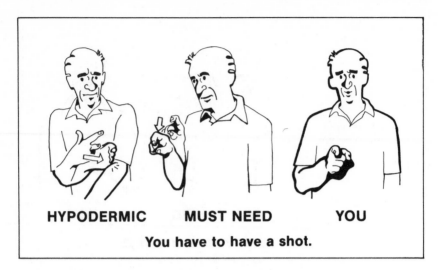

HYPODERMIC   MUST NEED   YOU

You have to have a shot.

The MUST sign may mean "need" or "should" and is done differently depending upon the meaning desired. If something is mandatory, then make one movement down. If something is optional but desirable, then make two gentle downward movements.

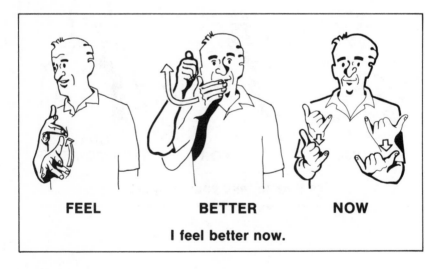

FEEL   BETTER   NOW

I feel better now.

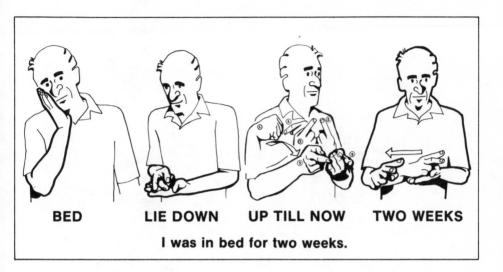

BED **LIE DOWN** **UP TILL NOW** **TWO WEEKS**

I was in bed for two weeks.

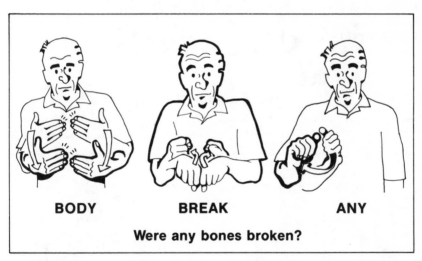

BODY **BREAK** **ANY**

Were any bones broken?

There is no standard sign for "bone," so the statement here is more generally read as, "Is anything in your body broken?" If you wish to sign "bone" specifically, then you must fingerspell it or find out what the local sign for it is.

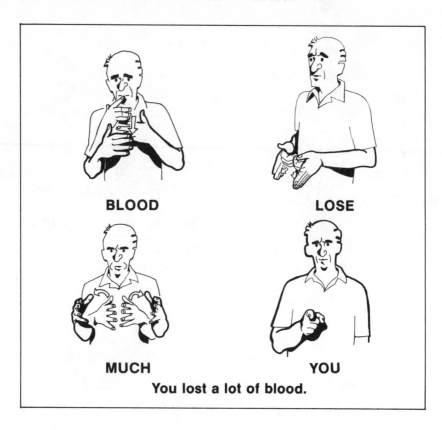

BLOOD

LOSE

MUCH

YOU

You lost a lot of blood.

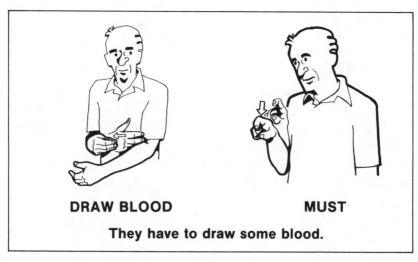

DRAW BLOOD

MUST

They have to draw some blood.

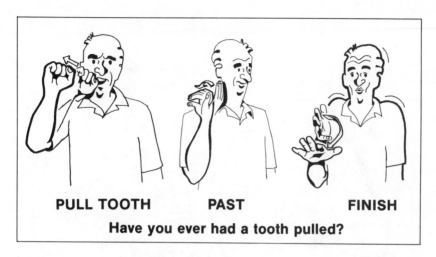

PULL TOOTH   PAST   FINISH
Have you ever had a tooth pulled?

The signs PAST and FINISH both refer to the past. Either one may be used alone here, but it is very common to see them both appear in a statement.

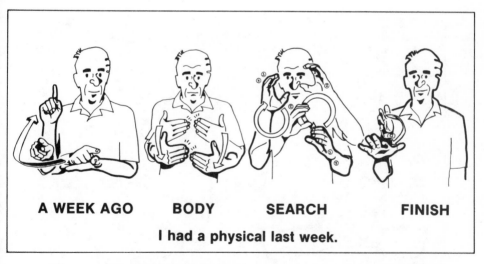

A WEEK AGO   BODY   SEARCH   FINISH
I had a physical last week.

The use of the FINISH sign here denotes the idea that I "already" had a physical last week.

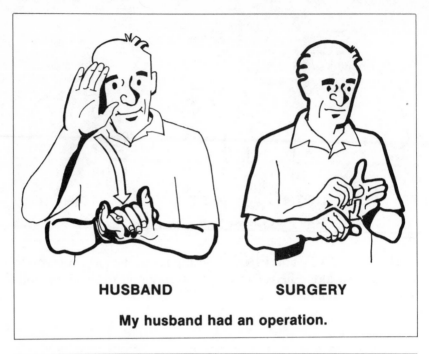

HUSBAND   **SURGERY**

My husband had an operation.

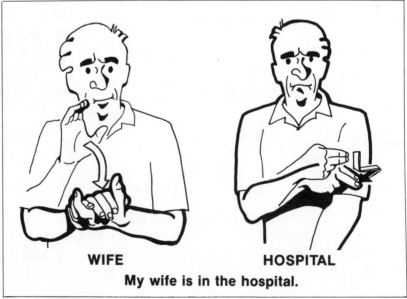

WIFE   **HOSPITAL**

My wife is in the hospital.

The HOSPITAL sign is made by drawing a cross on the sleeve.

PAST   **MONTH**   **FATHER**   **DIE**

My father passed away last month.

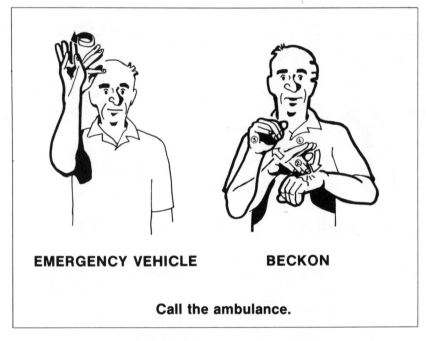

EMERGENCY VEHICLE   **BECKON**

Call the ambulance.

The sign for "ambulance" indicates the spinning red light on top of the vehicle and may refer to any emergency vehicle or just the flashing red light itself. Also, instead of the sign BECKON, you may sign PHONE.

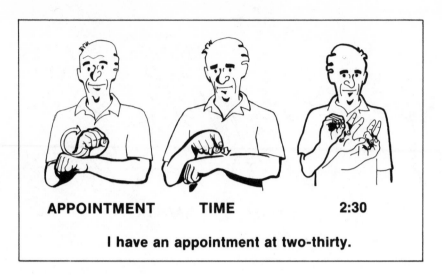

APPOINTMENT   **TIME**   **2:30**

I have an appointment at two-thirty.

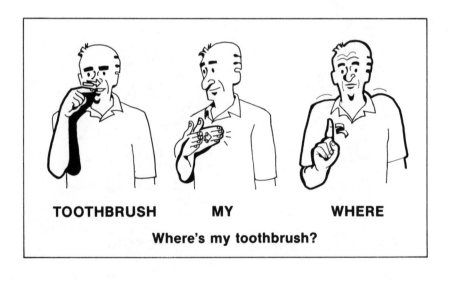

TOOTHBRUSH   **MY**   **WHERE**

Where's my toothbrush?

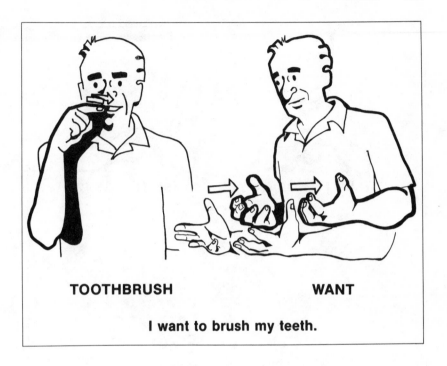

TOOTHBRUSH   **WANT**

I want to brush my teeth.

BATH   **SHOWER**   **FINISH**

I already took a bath/shower.

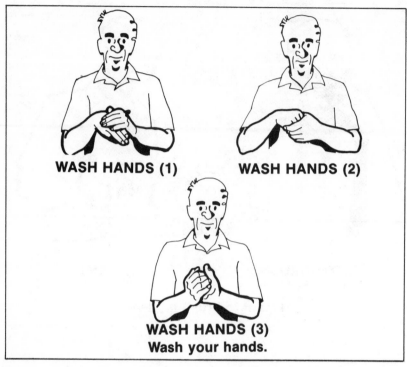

WASH HANDS (1)   **WASH HANDS (2)**

WASH HANDS (3)
Wash your hands.

The above sign, shown in three steps, is a mime of actually washing the hands, as the sign below is a mime of actually washing the face.

WASH FACE
Wash your face.

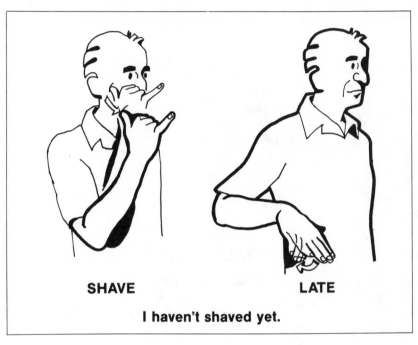

SHAVE   **LATE**

I haven't shaved yet.

HAIR DRYER   **LEND**

May I borrow your hair dryer?

BRUSH HAIR
Brush your hair.

COMB   LOSE
I lost my comb.

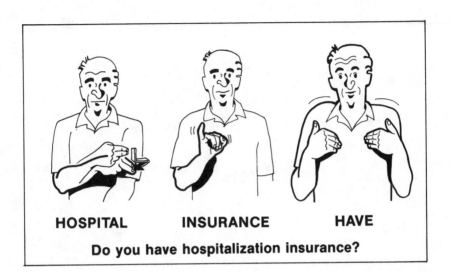

HOSPITAL   **INSURANCE**   **HAVE**

Do you have hospitalization insurance?

7
Weather

NOW   DAY   PRETTY

It's beautiful today.

SUN   **HOT**

The sun is hot.

SIT   **SUNRAY**   **PLEASE**

I enjoy sitting in the sun.

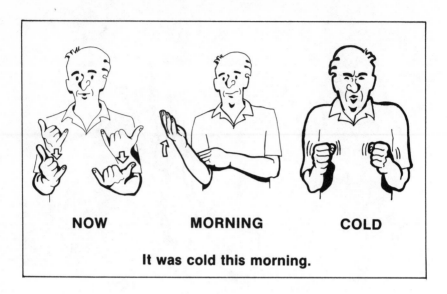

NOW   MORNING   COLD

It was cold this morning.

NOW   NIGHT   ICE

It will freeze tonight.

TOMORROW **SNOW** **MAYBE**

Maybe it will snow tomorrow.

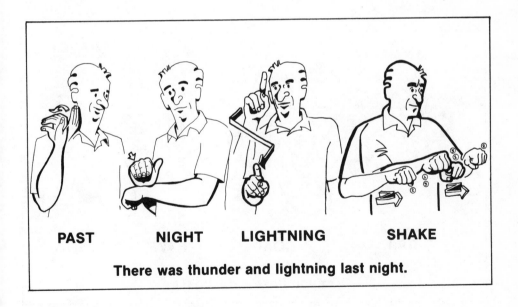

PAST **NIGHT** **LIGHTNING** **SHAKE**

There was thunder and lightning last night.

YESTERDAY   **RAIN**

It rained yesterday.

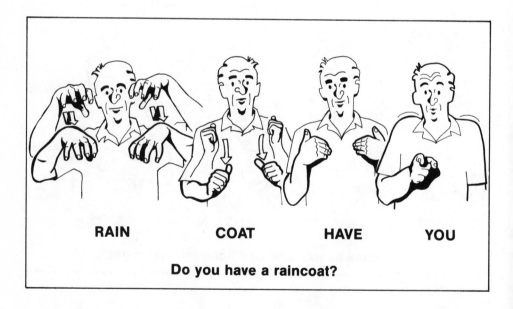

RAIN   **COAT**   **HAVE**   **YOU**

Do you have a raincoat?

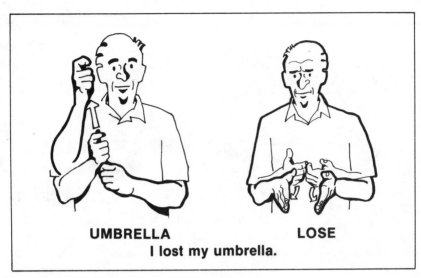

UMBRELLA   **LOSE**

I lost my umbrella.

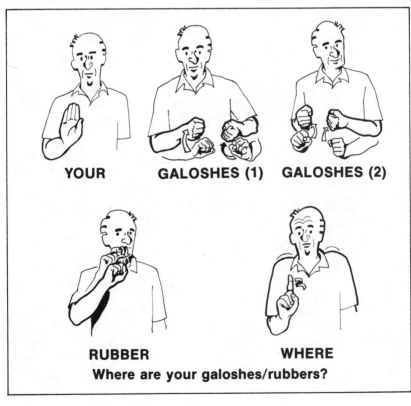

YOUR   **GALOSHES (1)**   **GALOSHES (2)**

RUBBER   **WHERE**

Where are your galoshes/rubbers?

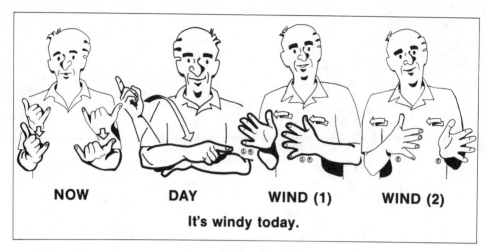

NOW   **DAY**   **WIND (1)**   **WIND (2)**

It's windy today.

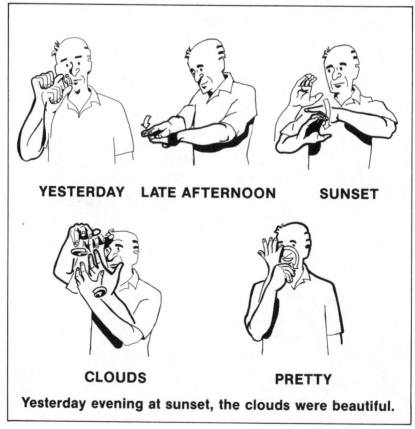

YESTERDAY   **LATE AFTERNOON**   **SUNSET**

CLOUDS   **PRETTY**

Yesterday evening at sunset, the clouds were beautiful.

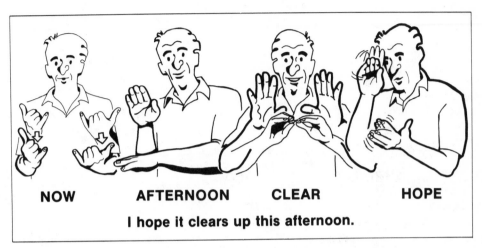

NOW   AFTERNOON   CLEAR   HOPE

I hope it clears up this afternoon.

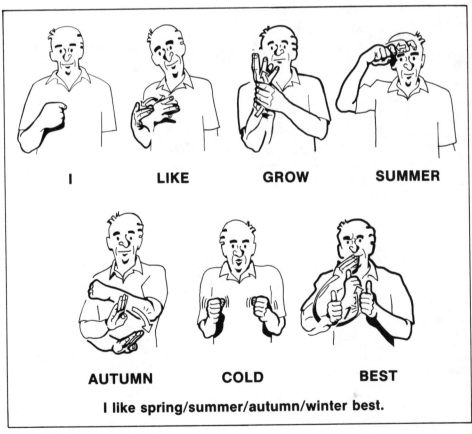

I   LIKE   GROW   SUMMER

AUTUMN   COLD   BEST

I like spring/summer/autumn/winter best.

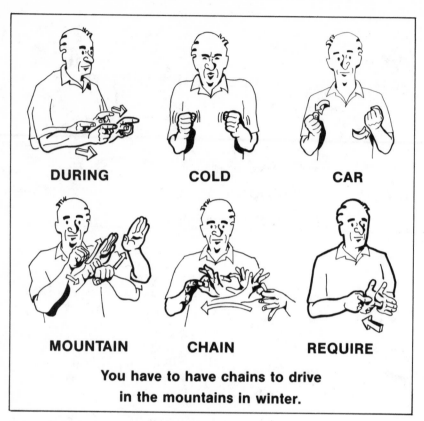

DURING   COLD   CAR

MOUNTAIN   CHAIN   REQUIRE

**You have to have chains to drive
in the mountains in winter.**

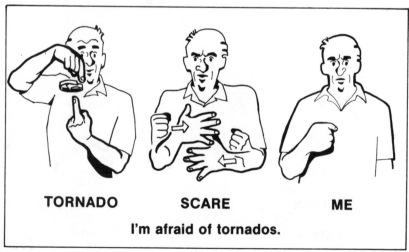

TORNADO   SCARE   ME

I'm afraid of tornados.

TEMPERATURE   **WHAT SHRUG**

What's the temperature?

SNOW   **MELT**   **FINISH**

Has the snow melted?

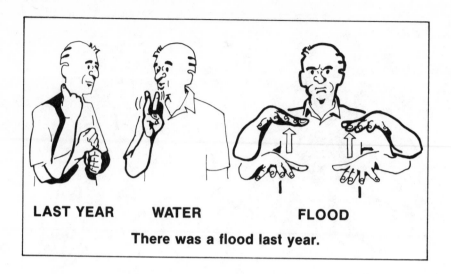

LAST YEAR   WATER   FLOOD

There was a flood last year.

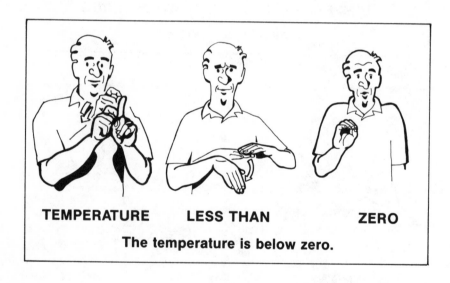

TEMPERATURE   LESS THAN   ZERO

The temperature is below zero.

EARTH   **SHAKE**

FINISH   **YOU**

Have you ever been in an earthquake?

There are no signs for "hurricane," "blizzard," "sleet," and "hail," so they must be fingerspelled.

8

Family

| YOUR | FATHER | FACE | NICE |

Your father is nice-looking.

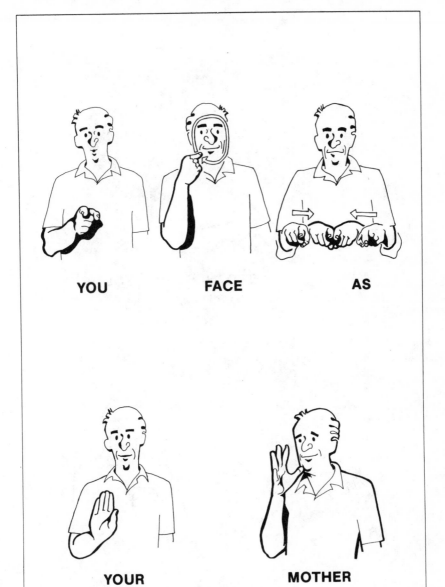

YOU FACE AS

YOUR MOTHER

You look like your mother.

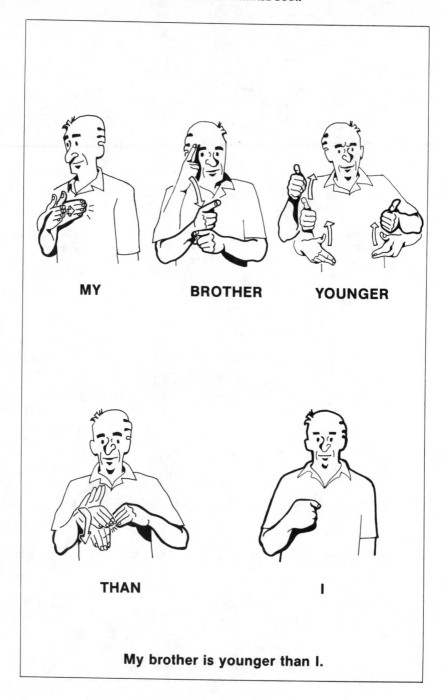

MY   **BROTHER**   **YOUNGER**

THAN   **I**

My brother is younger than I.

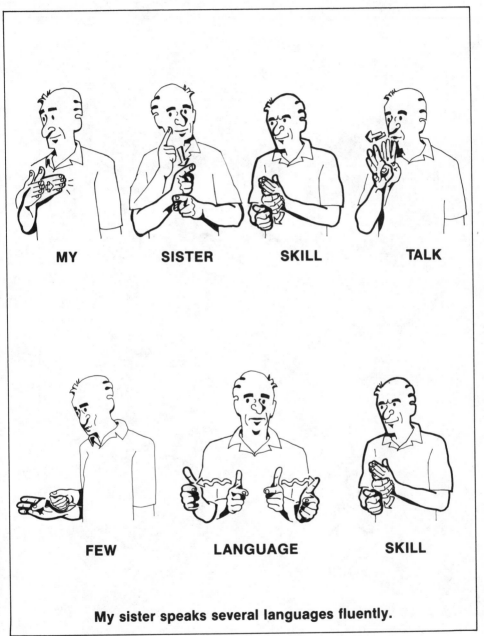

MY   **SISTER**   **SKILL**   **TALK**

FEW   **LANGUAGE**   **SKILL**

My sister speaks several languages fluently.

The repetition of a sign, as SKILL is repeated here, is a common practice.

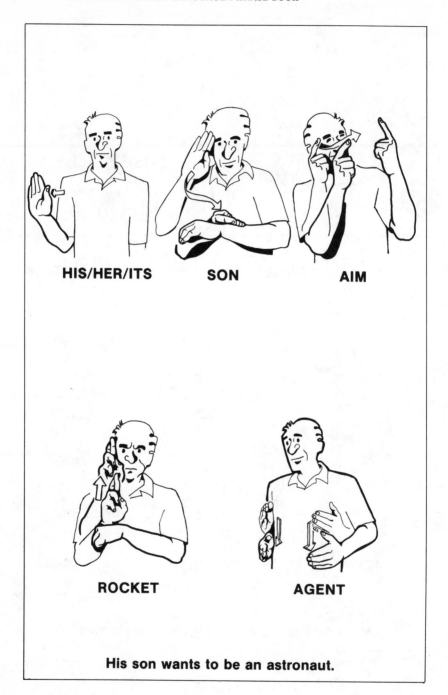

HIS/HER/ITS   **SON**   **AIM**

ROCKET   **AGENT**

His son wants to be an astronaut.

HIS/HER/ITS   **DAUGHTER**   **WORK**   **HERE**

Her daughter works here.

MY   **UNCLE**   **FARM**   **AGENT**

My uncle is a farmer.

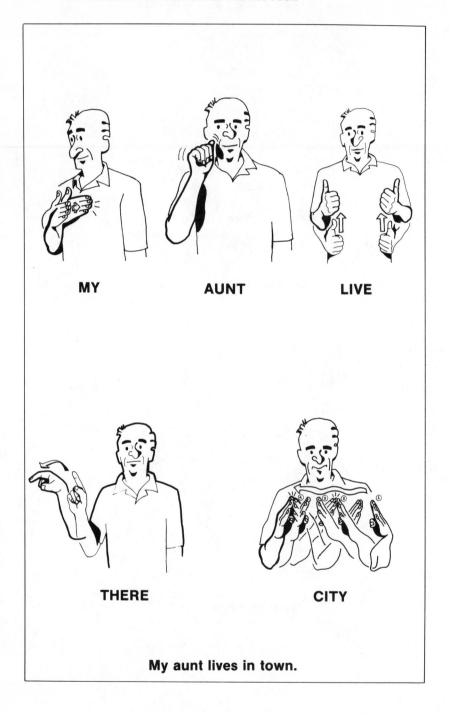

MY

AUNT

LIVE

THERE

CITY

My aunt lives in town.

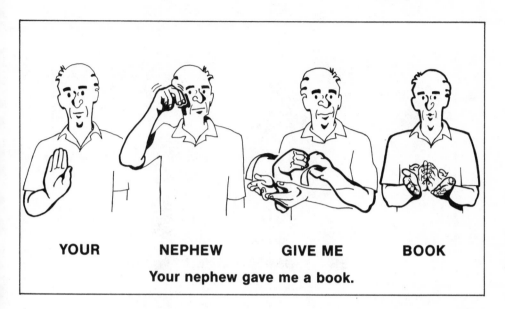

YOUR   NEPHEW   GIVE ME   BOOK

Your nephew gave me a book.

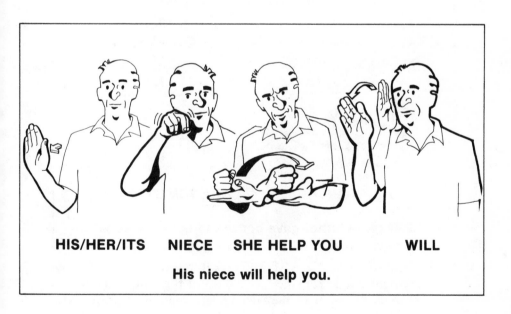

HIS/HER/ITS   NIECE   SHE HELP YOU   WILL

His niece will help you.

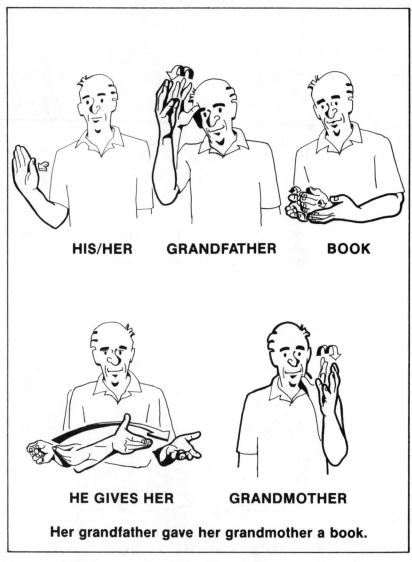

HIS/HER   GRANDFATHER   BOOK

HE GIVES HER   GRANDMOTHER

Her grandfather gave her grandmother a book.

Normally the sign GRANDMOTHER would have been made with the right hand, but since the action of the GIVE sign moves from the signer's right to the signer's left, making the GRAND-MOTHER sign with the left hand makes it visually clearer who is on which side. (For further explanation, see page 20, "Placement of Signs.")

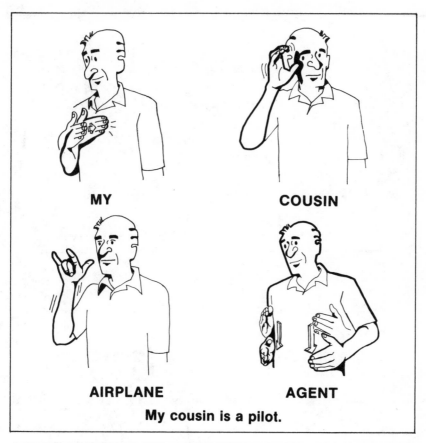

MY

COUSIN

AIRPLANE

AGENT

My cousin is a pilot.

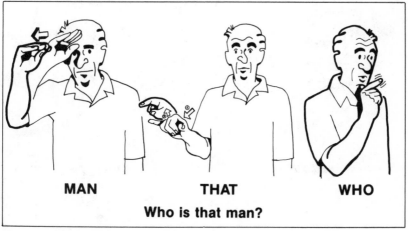

MAN

THAT

WHO

Who is that man?

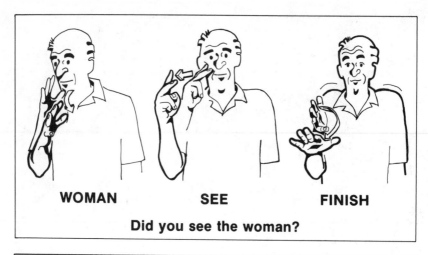

WOMAN   **SEE**   **FINISH**

Did you see the woman?

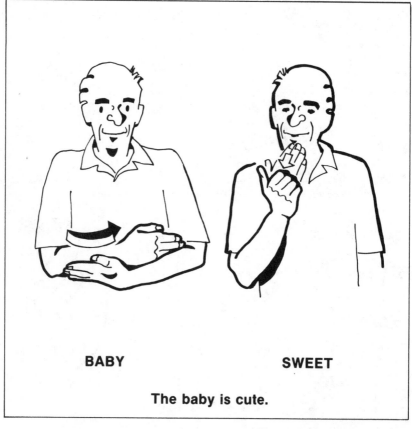

BABY   **SWEET**

The baby is cute.

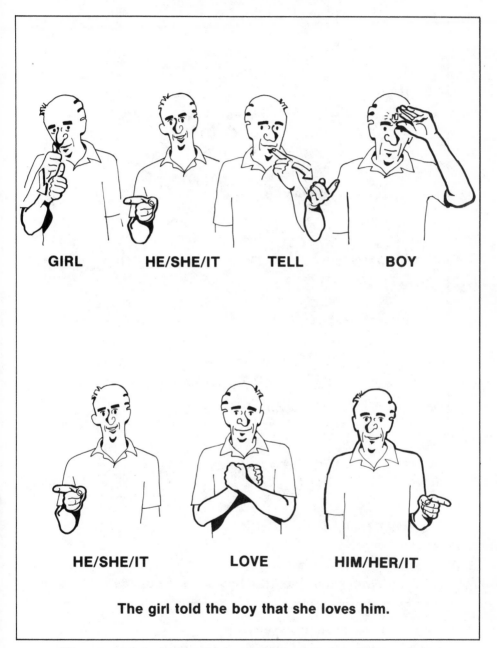

GIRL   **HE/SHE/IT**   **TELL**   **BOY**

HE/SHE/IT   **LOVE**   **HIM/HER/IT**

The girl told the boy that she loves him.

The use of both hands in making the sign helps reinforce visually who is doing what to whom.

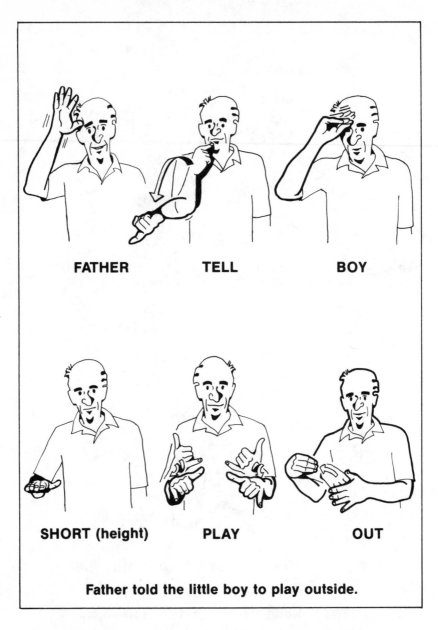

FATHER   **TELL**   **BOY**

SHORT (height)   **PLAY**   **OUT**

Father told the little boy to play outside.

The TELL sign moves downward to denote that the person being told is a child. The same thing occurs in the following sentence with the HER sign.

GIRL   SHORT (height)   HIS/HER/ITS

DOLL   BREAK

The little girl's doll is broken.

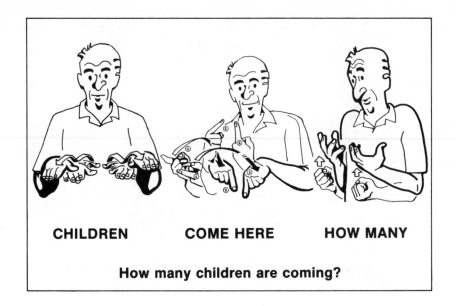

CHILDREN   COME HERE   HOW MANY

How many children are coming?

OUR   FAMILY   LARGE   SMALL

Our family is large/small.

PAST   **SUMMER**   **FAMILY**   **CONVENE**

We had a family reunion last summer.

The idea "we had" is understood and therefore not signed.

WE   **CONVENE**   **GRANDFATHER**

FARM   **THERE**

We met at Grandfather's farm.

9

School

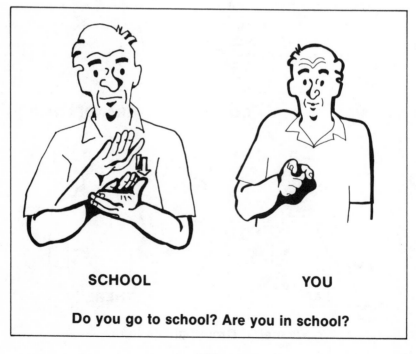

SCHOOL　　　　　　　　**YOU**

Do you go to school? Are you in school?

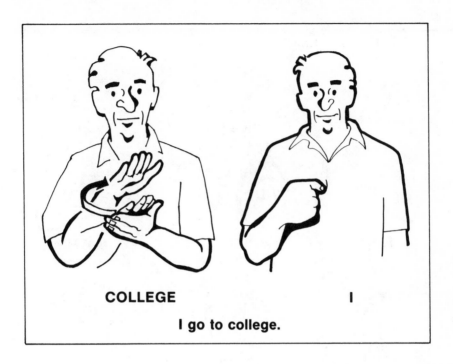

COLLEGE   **I**

I go to college.

I   **MAJOR**   **ENGLISH**

I'm majoring in English.

Additional vocabulary:

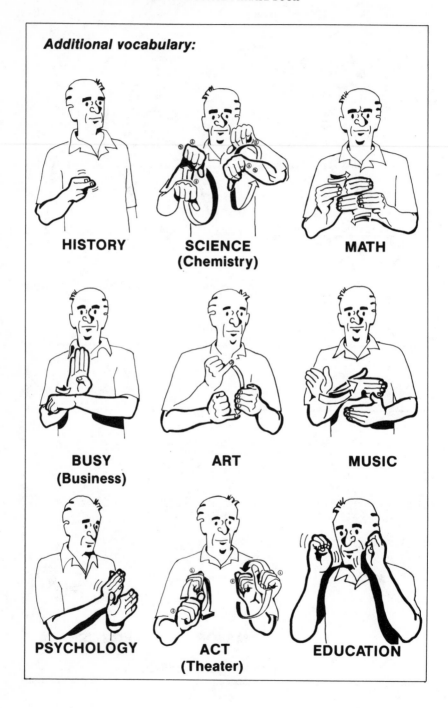

HISTORY

SCIENCE
(Chemistry)

MATH

BUSY
(Business)

ART

MUSIC

PSYCHOLOGY

ACT
(Theater)

EDUCATION

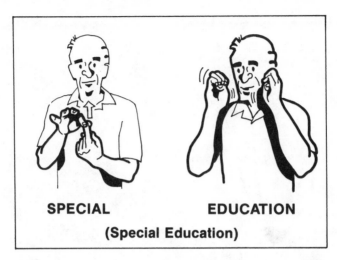

SPECIAL   **EDUCATION**

(Special Education)

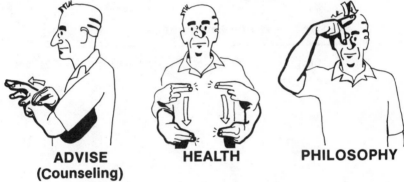

ADVISE   **HEALTH**   **PHILOSOPHY**

(Counseling)

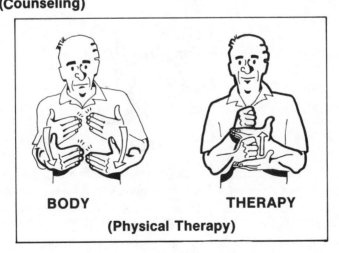

BODY   **THERAPY**

(Physical Therapy)

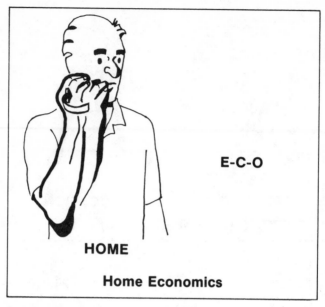

E-C-O

HOME

Home Economics

"Home Economics" is expressed by first signing HOME and then fingerspelling E-C-O.

COMPUTER

The sign for "computer" varies a good deal around the country, so check it out with your local deaf people.

Other academic fields are fingerspelled, either in full or in abbreviated form. "Physical Education" is "P–E;" "Library Science" is "L-S;" "Sociology" is "S-O-C," and so on.

NOW **SEMESTER** **LESSON**

LESSON (rear view) **TAKE UP** **WHAT SHRUG**

What course are you taking this semester?

LEARN **AGENT** **I**

I'm a student.

Additional vocabulary:

PREP

FRESHMAN

SOPHOMORE

JUNIOR

SENIOR

GRADUATE

LAST YEAR   **GRADUATE**   **I**

I graduated last year.

NOW   **GRADUATE**   **SCHOOL**   **I**

I'm in graduate school now.

STUDY   LIKE   I

I like to study.

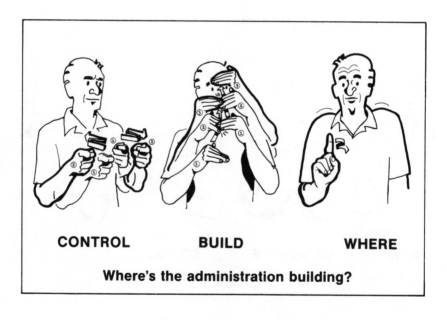

CONTROL   BUILD   WHERE

Where's the administration building?

LIBRARY   **GO TO**   **RESEARCH**   **MUST**

You've got to go to the library and do some research.

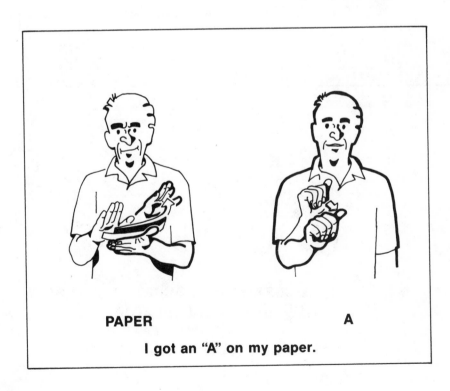

PAPER   **A**

I got an "A" on my paper.

STUDY   **ALL NIGHT**

I studied all night.

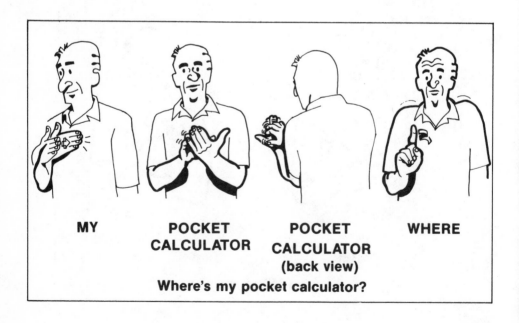

MY   **POCKET**   **POCKET**   **WHERE**
         CALCULATOR   **CALCULATOR**
                          (back view)

Where's my pocket calculator?

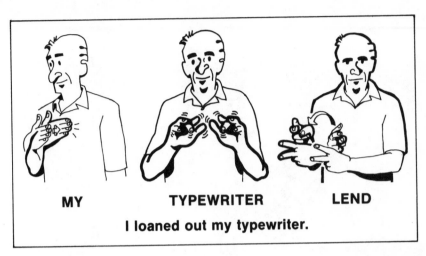

MY   **TYPEWRITER**   **LEND**

I loaned out my typewriter.

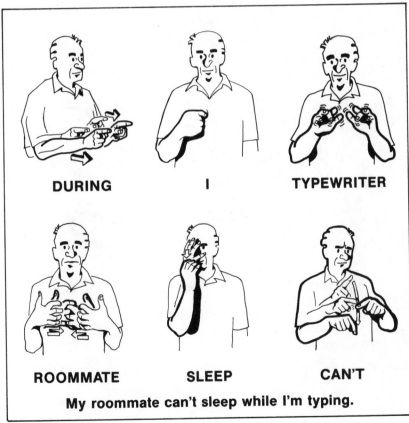

DURING   **I**   **TYPEWRITER**

ROOMMATE   **SLEEP**   **CAN'T**

My roommate can't sleep while I'm typing.

QUERY

I have a question.

QUERY   FINISH   YOU

Did you ask him?

TEACH   **QUERY ME**

The teacher asked me a lot of questions.

The repetition of the QUERY sign using both hands indicates that many questions were asked.

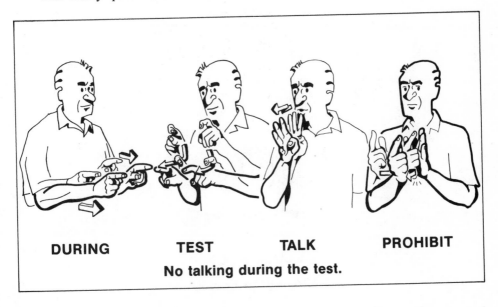

DURING   **TEST**   **TALK**   **PROHIBIT**

No talking during the test.

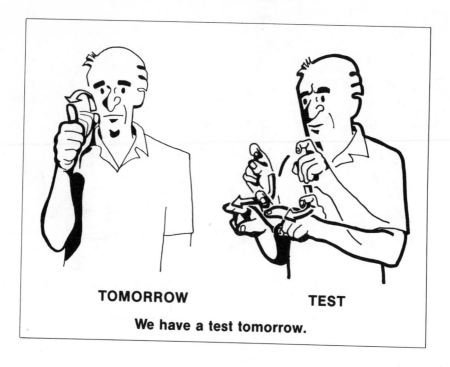

TOMORROW   **TEST**

We have a test tomorrow.

CLOSE BOOK

Close your books.

OPEN BOOK

Open your books.

WRITE   **START**

Begin writing.

WRITE   **STOP**

Stop writing.

WRITE   **LOSE**

I lost my pencil.

The sign WRITE also stands for "pen," "pencil," and any other writing instrument.

WRITE   **AWFUL (1)**   **AWFUL (2)**   **YOU**

Your writing is terrible.

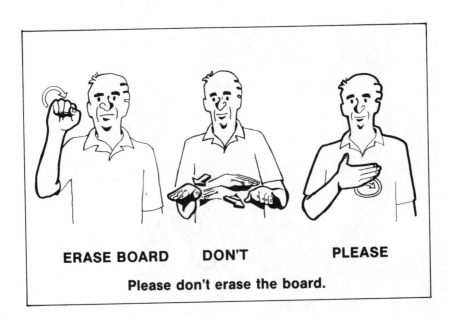

ERASE BOARD   **DON'T**   **PLEASE**

Please don't erase the board.

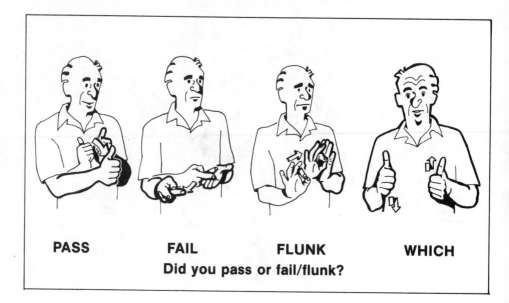

PASS   **FAIL**   **FLUNK**   **WHICH**

Did you pass or fail/flunk?

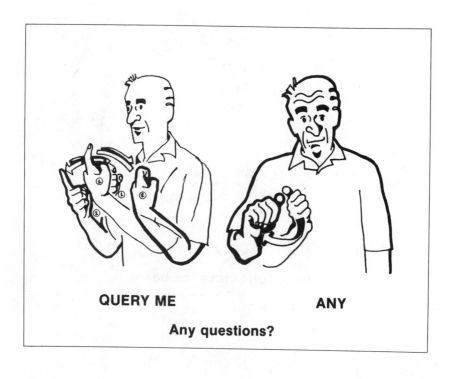

QUERY ME   **ANY**

Any questions?

PAPER   **GIVE ME**   **LATE**

You haven't turned in your paper to me yet.

In order to sign GIVE, reverse the movement of the GIVE ME sign.

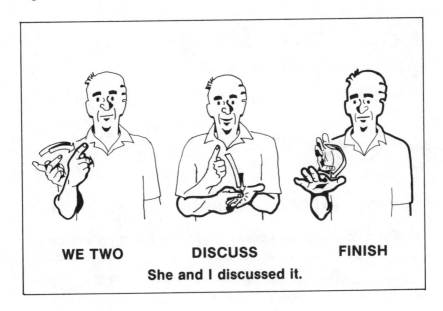

WE TWO   **DISCUSS**   **FINISH**

She and I discussed it.

BREAK

Let's take a break.

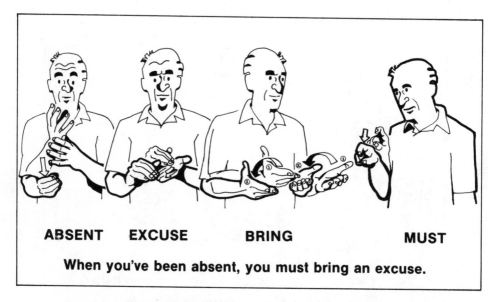

ABSENT   EXCUSE   BRING   MUST

When you've been absent, you must bring an excuse.

Conditional statements such as "When you've eaten, you may go" or "If you're good, I'll tell you" are usually changed to questions. In the sentence shown above, the ABSENT sign is made with a questioning expression.

10

Food and Drink

EAT   FINISH

Have you eaten? Did you eat? Are you finished eating?

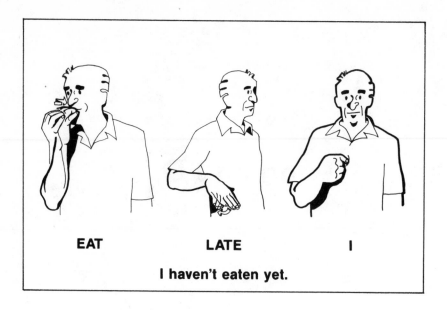

EAT   **LATE**   **I**

I haven't eaten yet.

HE/SHE/IT   **EAT**   **TOO MUCH**

He eats too much.

HUNGER   **YOU**

Are you hungry?

YOU AND I   **GO TO**   **RESTAURANT**

Let's you and I go to a restaurant.

ORDER   **WHAT SHRUG**

What are you going to order?

COCKTAIL   **WANT**

Do you want a cocktail?

RED

WHITE

WINE

WANT

WHICH

Do you want red or white wine?

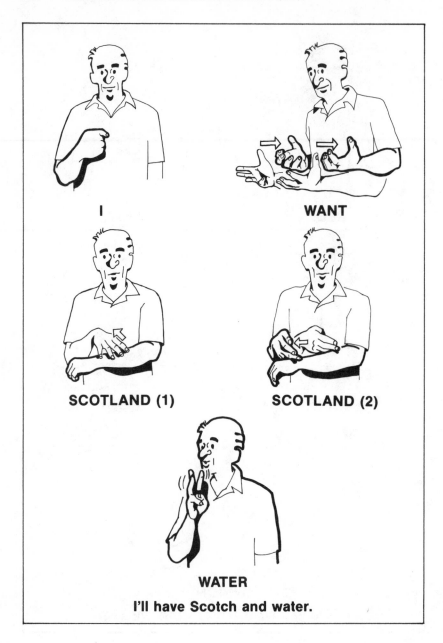

I

WANT

SCOTLAND (1)

SCOTLAND (2)

WATER

I'll have Scotch and water.

TALL (glass)

GLASS

COKE

PEPSI

WANT

I want a tall Coke/Pepsi.

Coke and Pepsi are the only soft drinks with signs; all others are fingerspelled. The same applies to Scotch and other liquors and mixed drinks. Only Scotch has a sign; the rest are fingerspelled.

SOFT DRINK (1) SOFT DRINK (2)   WANT

Do you want a soft drink?

BEER   VARIOUS   HAVE

They have a lot of different beers.

WHISKEY   **NEVER**   **HE**

He never drinks whiskey.

SANDWICH   HAMBURGER   LIKE   I

I like sandwiches and hamburgers.

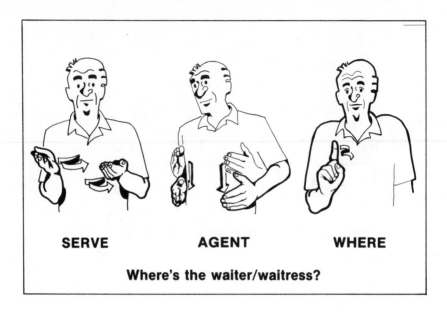

SERVE   AGENT   WHERE

Where's the waiter/waitress?

SERVE   LOUSY

The service is lousy.

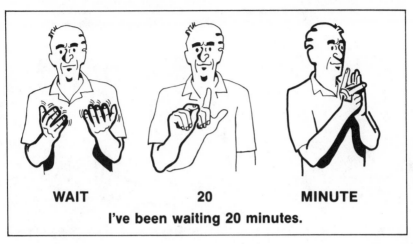

WAIT   **20**   **MINUTE**

I've been waiting 20 minutes.

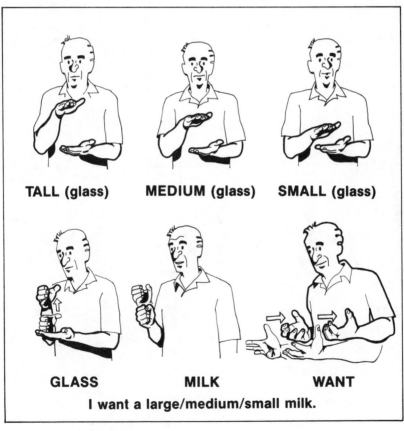

TALL (glass)   **MEDIUM (glass)**   **SMALL (glass)**

GLASS   **MILK**   **WANT**

I want a large/medium/small milk.

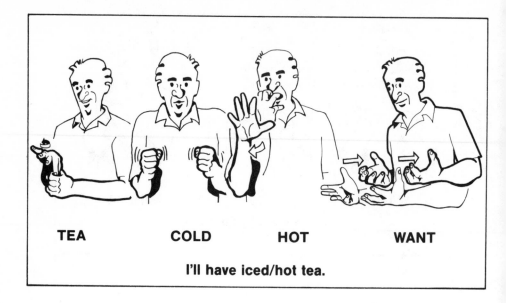

TEA   COLD   HOT   WANT

I'll have iced/hot tea.

EAT   FINISH   COFFEE   WANT

I'll have coffee after I eat.

MILK   CREAM   SWEET   WANT

Do your want milk/cream and sugar?

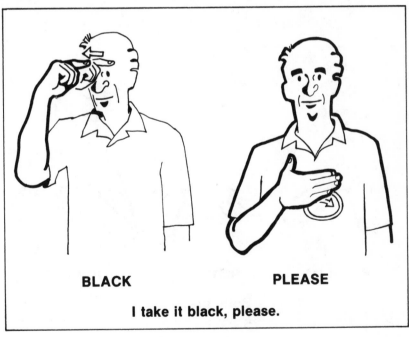

BLACK   PLEASE

I take it black, please.

SWEET   **ONLY**   **PLEASE**

Sugar only, please.

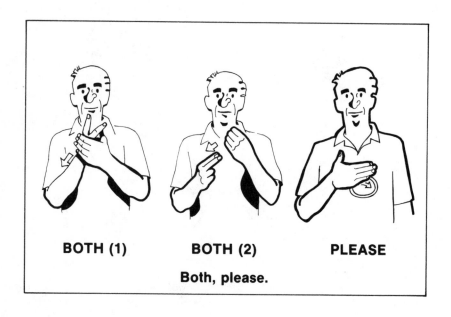

BOTH (1)   **BOTH (2)**   **PLEASE**

Both, please.

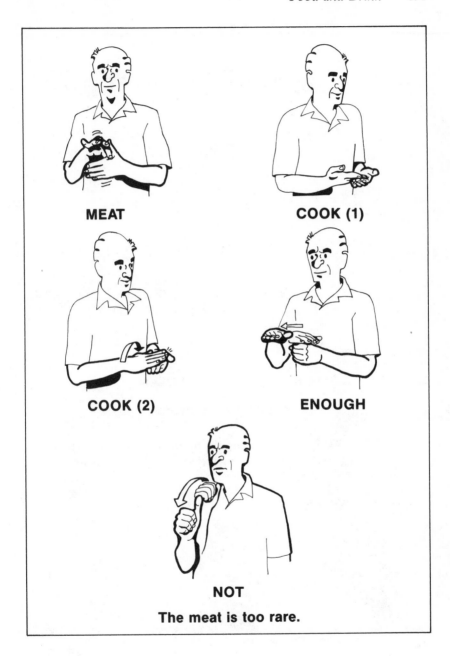

MEAT

COOK (1)

COOK (2)

ENOUGH

NOT

The meat is too rare.

V-E-G

COOK (1)

COOK (2)

TOO MUCH

The vegetables are overdone.

Fingerspell "V-E-G" at the beginning of the sentence. Most vegetables, fruits, and meats are fingerspelled. Those that have signs follow.

Additional vocabulary:

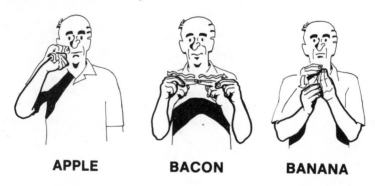

APPLE   **BACON**   **BANANA**

CABBAGE/LETTUCE   CARROT   CHICKEN (A-1)

CHICKEN (A-2)*   CHICKEN (B)   COCONUT

CORN   FISH   LEMON

*This is the sign for "BIRD," but it is often used for "chicken."

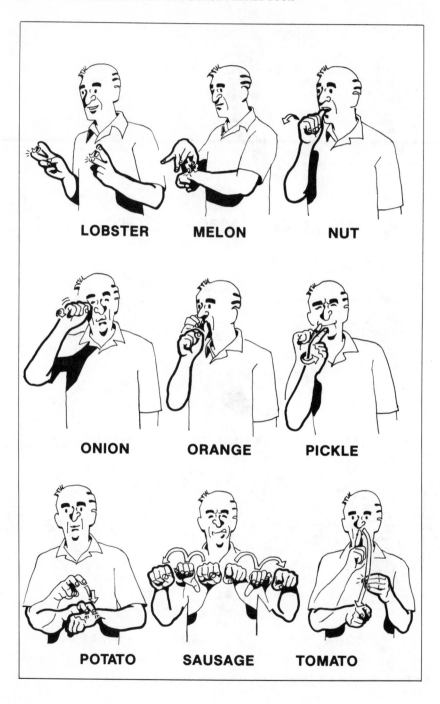

LOBSTER   **MELON**   **NUT**

ONION   **ORANGE**   **PICKLE**

POTATO   **SAUSAGE**   **TOMATO**

EAT   **DELICIOUS**

The food is delicious.

The following signs are for describing how you want your eggs.

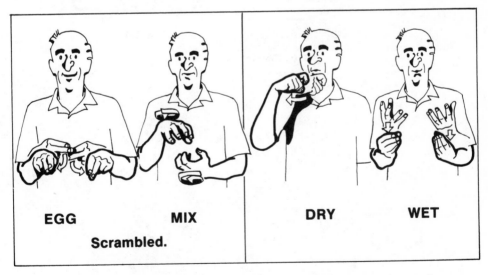

EGG   **MIX**   **DRY**   **WET**

Scrambled.

To indicate whether you want your scrambled eggs moist or dry, sign WET or DRY after EGG MIX.

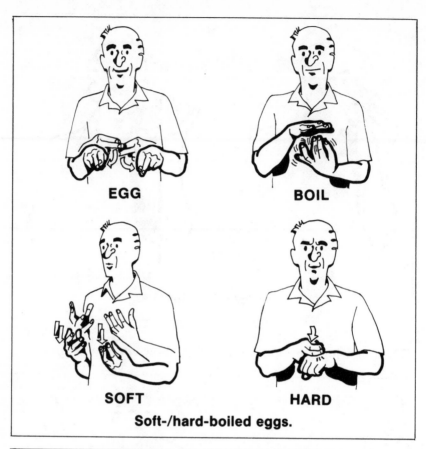

EGG

BOIL

SOFT

HARD

Soft-/hard-boiled eggs.

EGG

THUMB UP

Eggs sunny side up.

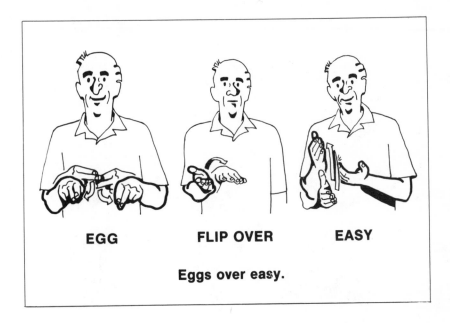

EGG   **FLIP OVER**   **EASY**

Eggs over easy.

Additional vocabulary:

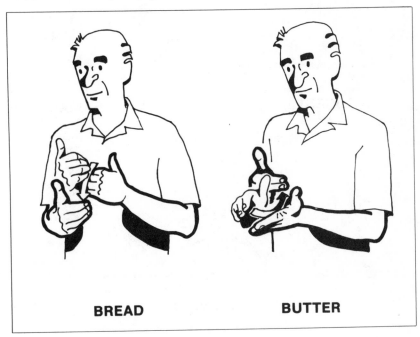

BREAD   **BUTTER**

CAKE (1)   CAKE (2)   CATSUP

DESSERT   FORK   GREASE

ICE CREAM   KNIFE   PEPPER

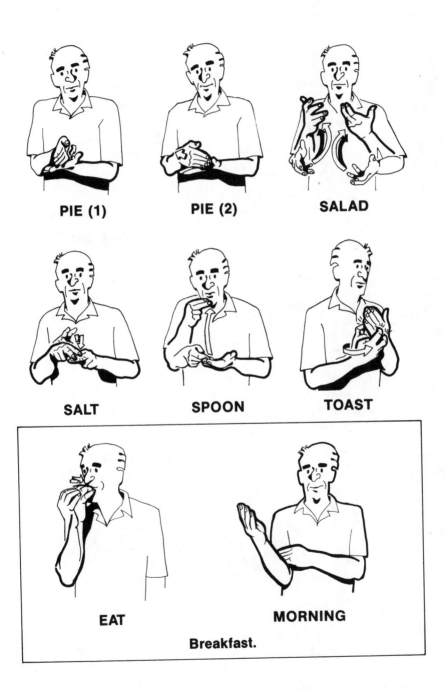

PIE (1)　　**PIE (2)**　　**SALAD**

SALT　　**SPOON**　　**TOAST**

EAT　　**MORNING**

Breakfast.

EAT   **NOON**

Lunch.

EAT   **NIGHT**

Supper/Dinner.

11

Clothing

GO TO **BUY** **MUST**
I have to go shopping.

The BUY sign is repeated to convey the idea "shopping."

NOW   NIGHT   DRESS   WHAT SHRUG

What are you wearing tonight?

DRESS   COLOR   ODD

That dress is an odd color.

DRESS   **DIRTY**   **HAVE**

Do you have any dirty clothes?

WASHING MACHINE   **MUST**

I need to do some laundry.

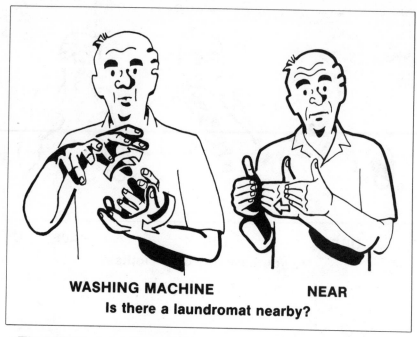

WASHING MACHINE   **NEAR**
Is there a laundromat nearby?

The NEAR sign is done so that the hands do not actually touch each other.

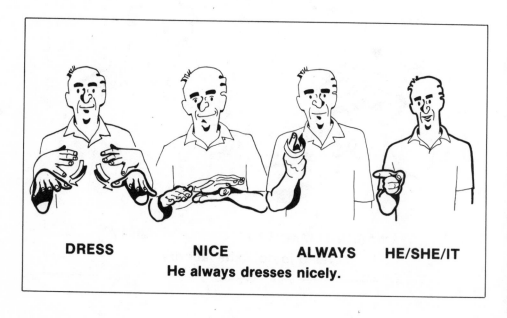

DRESS   **NICE**   **ALWAYS**   **HE/SHE/IT**
He always dresses nicely.

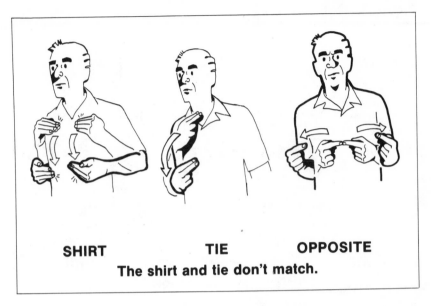

SHIRT **TIE** **OPPOSITE**

The shirt and tie don't match.

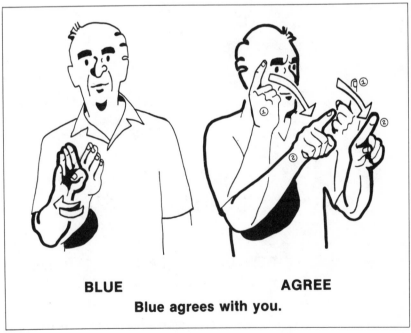

BLUE **AGREE**

Blue agrees with you.

Ordinarily the AGREE sign just moves downward, but when it is used in the expression above, it must move toward the watcher.

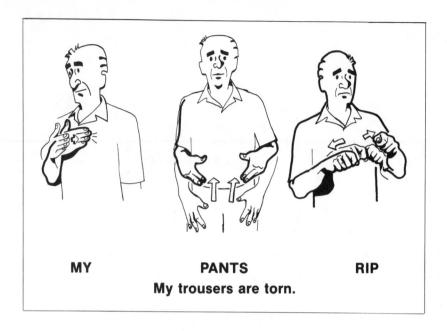

MY   PANTS   RIP
My trousers are torn.

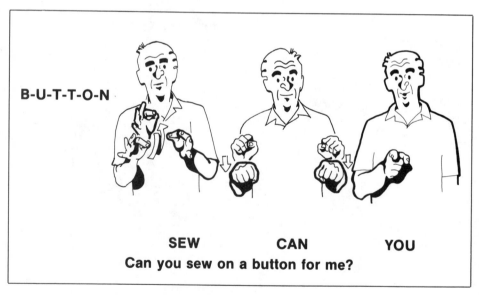

B-U-T-T-O-N

SEW   CAN   YOU
Can you sew on a button for me?

Fingerspell BUTTON at the beginning of the sentence before the sign SEW.

BOW TIE   **TIE KNOT**   **CAN'T**

I can't tie a bow tie.

NOW   **DAY**   **MOST**

WOMAN   **USE**   **SLACKS**

Most women wear slacks nowadays.

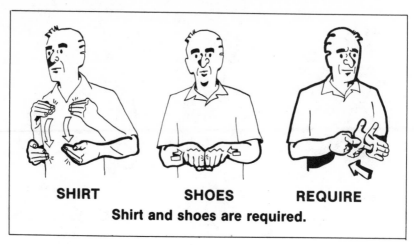

SHIRT   **SHOES**   **REQUIRE**

Shirt and shoes are required.

DURING   **SUMMER**   **SHORTS**

EVERY DAY   **I**

I wear shorts every day in the summer.

SHIRT   **WASH CLOTHES**   **MUST**

I need to wash out my shirt.

SOCKS   **SAME**   **NOT**

Your socks don't match.

MY   **HAT**   **GRAB**   **WHO**

Who took my hat?

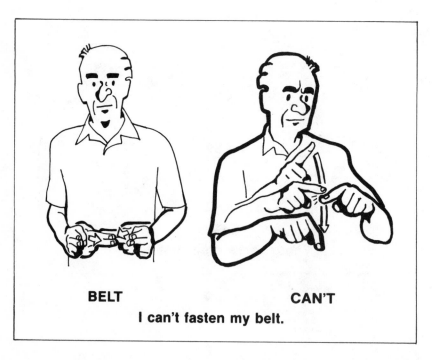

BELT   **CAN'T**

I can't fasten my belt.

COAT

PUT

CLEANERS

FINISH

SHORTER SLEEVE

When I took my coat to the cleaners, it shrunk.

12

Sports and Recreation

PLAY   **BASEBALL**   **LIKE**

Do you like to play baseball?

Additional vocabulary:

| BASKETBALL | BILLIARDS | CARDS |

| CHECKERS | DOMINOES | ELECTRONIC GAMES |

| FOOTBALL | GOLF | HANDBALL |

SOCCER

TABLE TENNIS

TENNIS

VOLLEYBALL

EVERY DAY   **RUN**   **I**

I run every day.

MOUNTAIN **GO TO** **FISHING** **PLEASE**

I enjoy going to the mountains to fish.

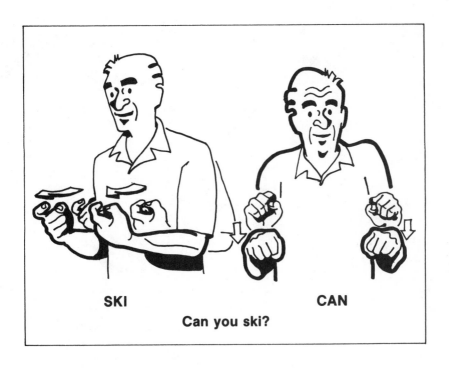

SKI **CAN**

Can you ski?

PAST   SUMMER   TENT   I

I went camping last summer.

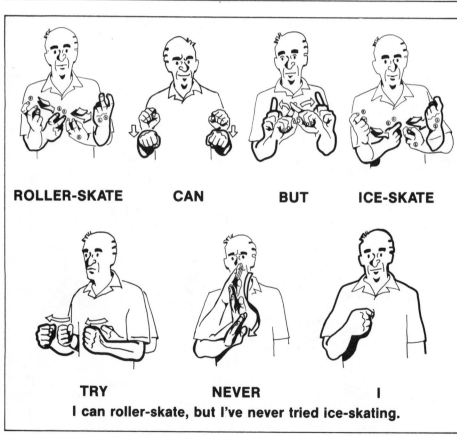

ROLLER-SKATE   CAN   BUT   ICE-SKATE

TRY   NEVER   I

I can roller-skate, but I've never tried ice-skating.

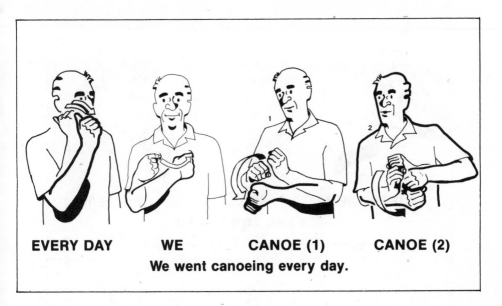

EVERY DAY   **WE**   **CANOE (1)**   **CANOE (2)**

We went canoeing every day.

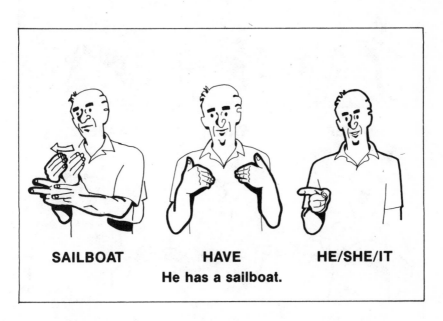

SAILBOAT   **HAVE**   **HE/SHE/IT**

He has a sailboat.

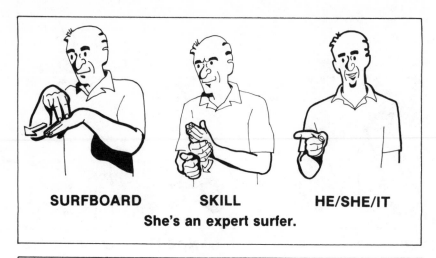

SURFBOARD   SKILL   HE/SHE/IT
She's an expert surfer.

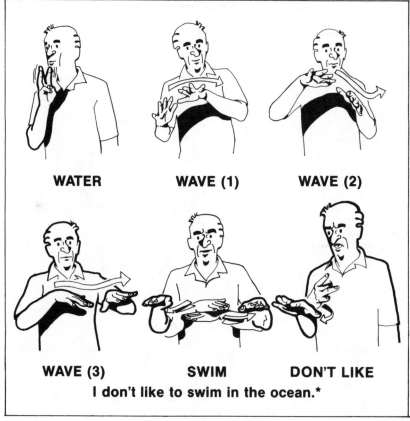

WATER   WAVE (1)   WAVE (2)

WAVE (3)   SWIM   DON'T LIKE
I don't like to swim in the ocean.*

*It takes four signs to express "OCEAN"—WATER, WAVE (1), WAVE (2), and WAVE (3).

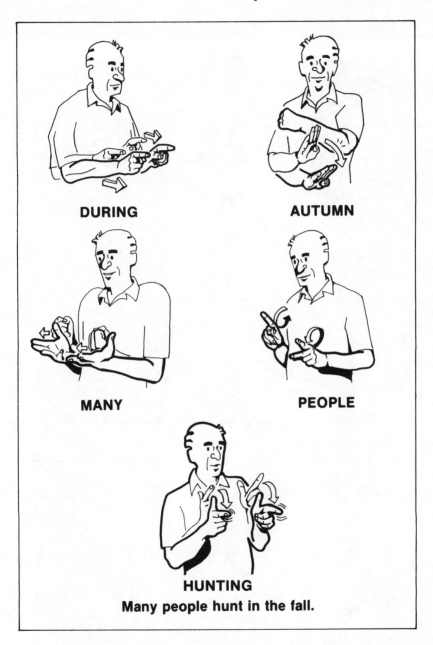

DURING

AUTUMN

MANY

PEOPLE

HUNTING

Many people hunt in the fall.

HORSE   COMPETE   BET

CRAZY   HE/SHE/IT

He's crazy about betting on the horses.

RIDE HORSE   LOVE   HE/SHE/IT

She loves to ride horses.

CHAIN
(Olympics)   **COMPETE**   **HOPE**   **HE/SHE/IT**

He hopes to compete in the Olympics.

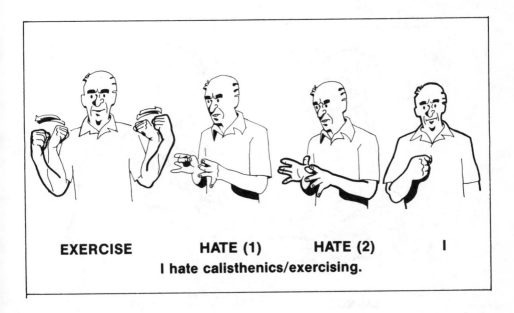

EXERCISE   **HATE (1)**   **HATE (2)**   **I**

I hate calisthenics/exercising.

DURING   LOAF   DO-DO   WHAT SHRUG
What do you do in your spare time?

DANCE   LIKE
Do you like to dance?

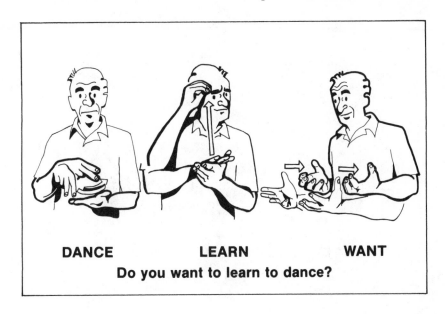

DANCE **LEARN** **WANT**
Do you want to learn to dance?

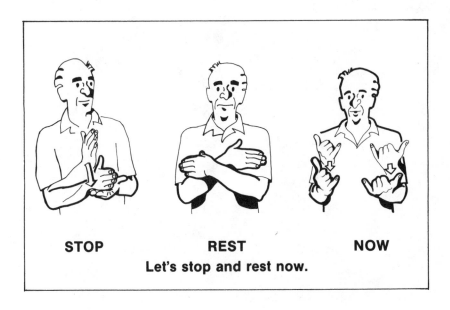

STOP **REST** **NOW**
Let's stop and rest now.

WEEKLY   **BOWL**   I
I go bowling every week.

13
Travel

ONLY   DAY   I

GO TO   AFRICA

Someday I'm going to Africa.

Additional vocabulary:

AMERICA   **AUSTRALIA**   **CANADA**

CHINA   **DENMARK**   **EGYPT**

ENGLAND   **EUROPE**   **FINLAND**

FRANCE   **GERMANY**   **GREECE**

HAWAII   **HOLLAND**   **INDIA**

IRELAND   **ISRAEL**   **ITALY**

JAPAN   MEXICO   NORWAY

POLAND   RUSSIA   SPAIN

SCOTLAND (1)   SCOTLAND (2)   SWEDEN

TOUCH   **FINISH**   **JAPAN**   **YOU**

Have you ever been to Japan?

NOW   **NIGHT**   **AIRPLANE**   **NEW YORK**

I'm flying to New York tonight.

Almost every city has a sign, or a fingerspelled abbreviation. Often, however, the sign is either not common outside the state or it is the same sign for another city in another state. For example,

Berkeley and Boston share the same sign. Therefore, one must inquire of local deaf people how the cities in their state are signed. A few cities do have signs that are used all over the country. New York is one such city, and others are shown below:

ATLANTA   CHICAGO   MILWAUKEE

NEW ORLEANS   PHILADELPHIA   PITTSBURGH

SAN FRANCISCO   **WASHINGTON**

San Francisco is abbreviated to "SF," and so are many other cities. Take care with Los Angeles, since its abbreviation can also mean Louisiana.

PACK BAGS   **FINISH**
Are your bags packed?

I   BRING   AIRPLANE
I'll take you to the airport.

AIRPLANE   NAME   WHICH
Which airline are you taking?

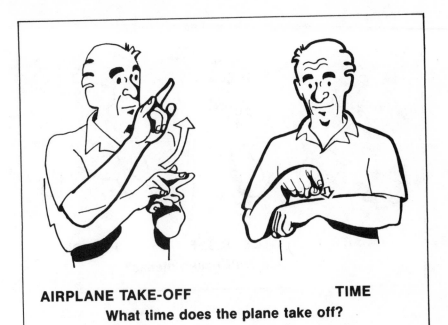

AIRPLANE TAKE-OFF   **TIME**

What time does the plane take off?

TICKET   **HAVE**

Do you have your ticket?

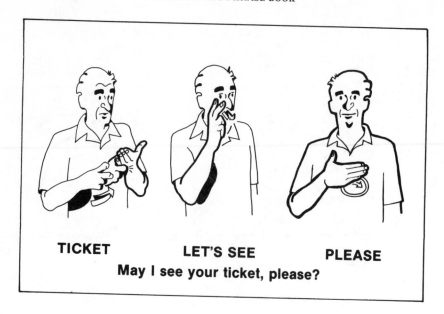

TICKET   LET'S SEE   PLEASE

May I see your ticket, please?

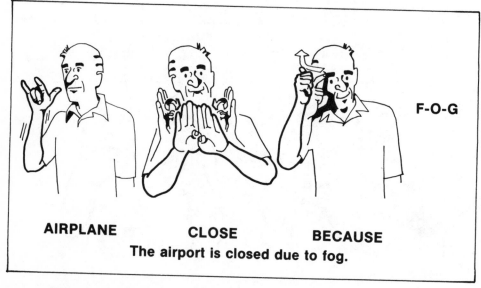

F-O-G

AIRPLANE   CLOSE   BECAUSE

The airport is closed due to fog.

There is no sign for "fog," so fingerspell it at the end of the sentence, after the sign BECAUSE.

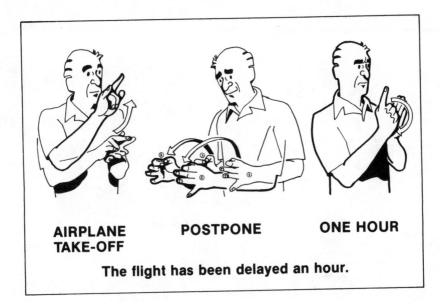

AIRPLANE TAKE-OFF   **POSTPONE**   **ONE HOUR**

The flight has been delayed an hour.

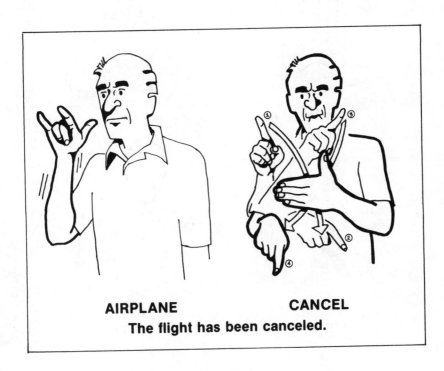

AIRPLANE   **CANCEL**

The flight has been canceled.

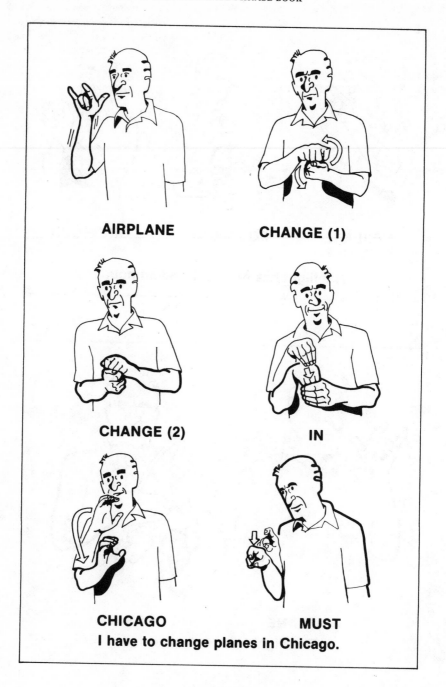

AIRPLANE

CHANGE (1)

CHANGE (2)

IN

CHICAGO

MUST

I have to change planes in Chicago.

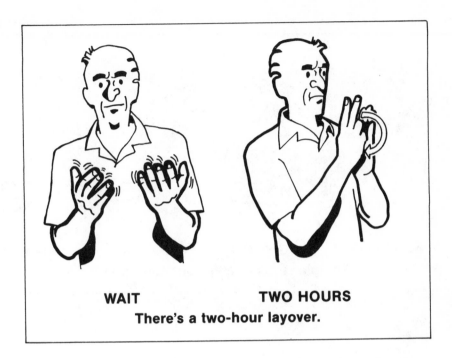

WAIT   **TWO HOURS**
There's a two-hour layover.

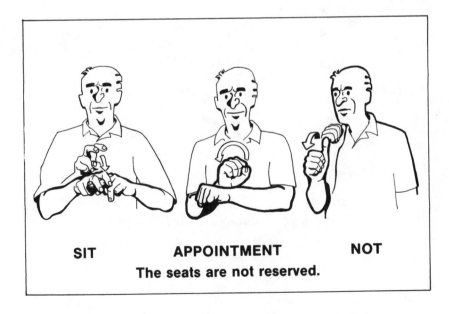

SIT   **APPOINTMENT**   **NOT**
The seats are not reserved.

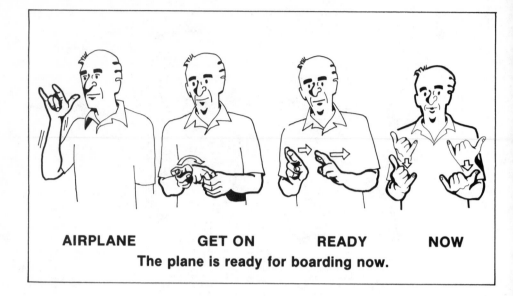

AIRPLANE   GET ON   READY   NOW

The plane is ready for boarding now.

LUGGAGE   TICKET   FINISH

Have you checked your luggage?

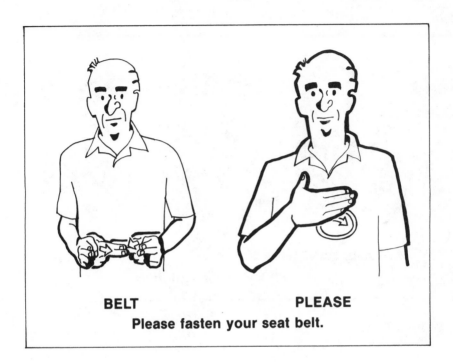

BELT   **PLEASE**

Please fasten your seat belt.

MAGAZINE   **NEWSPAPER (1)**   **NEWSPAPER (2)**   **WANT**

Would you like a magazine or newspaper?

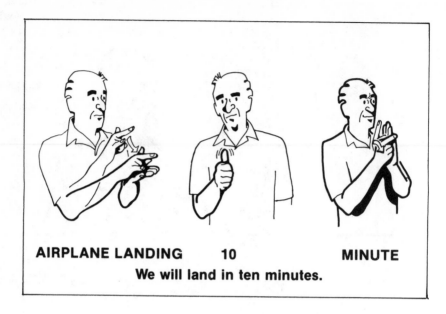

AIRPLANE LANDING   10   MINUTE
We will land in ten minutes.

ONLY   MEET   YOU
Is somebody meeting you?

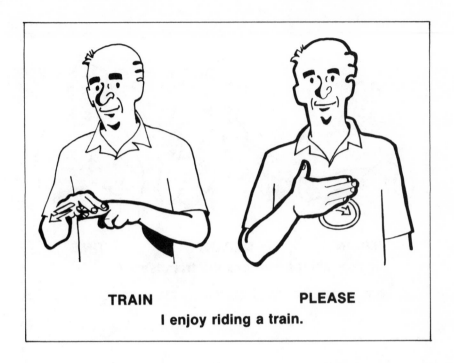

TRAIN **PLEASE**

I enjoy riding a train.

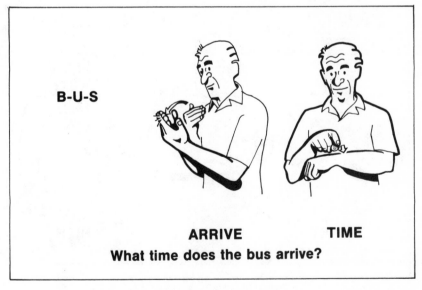

B-U-S

ARRIVE **TIME**

What time does the bus arrive?

There is no sign for "bus," so fingerspell it at the beginning of the sentence before the sign ARRIVE.

TRAIN   DEPART   TIME
What time does the train leave?

TICKET   BUY   FINISH
Have you bought your ticket?

GO TO   **HOTEL**   **BATH**

I'm going to the hotel to take a bath.

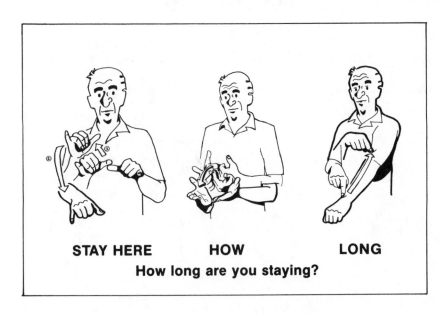

STAY HERE   **HOW**   **LONG**

How long are you staying?

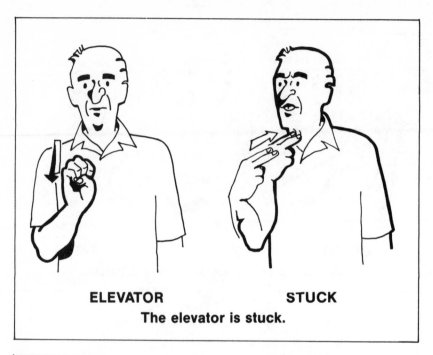

ELEVATOR   **STUCK**

The elevator is stuck.

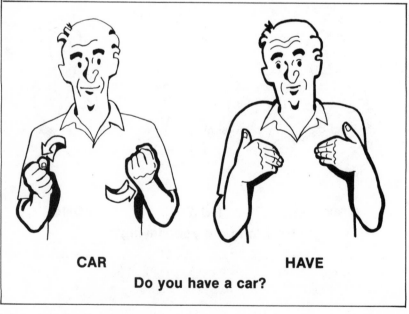

CAR   **HAVE**

Do you have a car?

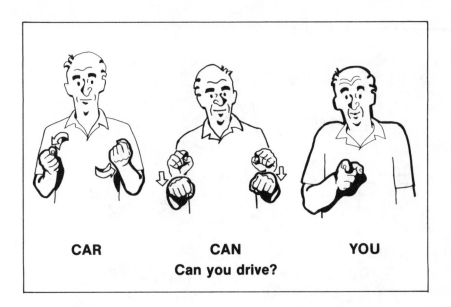

CAR   **CAN**   **YOU**

Can you drive?

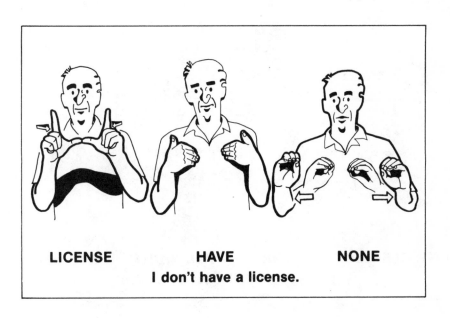

LICENSE   **HAVE**   **NONE**

I don't have a license.

SHIFT   KNOW   HOW
Do you know how to use a manual shift?

VEHICLE (park)   HERE   ALL NIGHT   PROHIBIT
It's illegal to park here overnight.

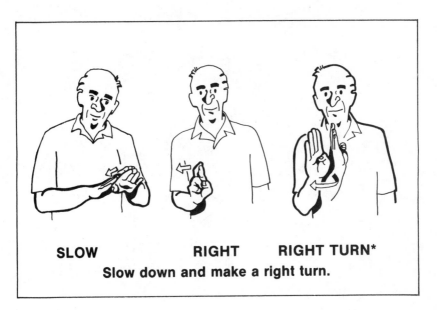

SLOW   **RIGHT**   **RIGHT TURN***

Slow down and make a right turn.

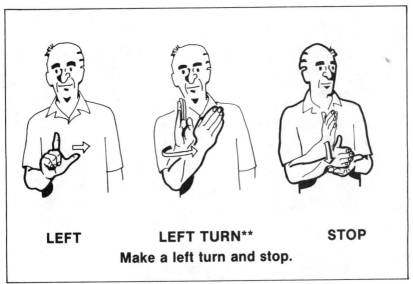

LEFT   **LEFT TURN****   **STOP**

Make a left turn and stop.

---

*"RIGHT" means "as opposed to left," but "RIGHT TURN" is one sign.

**"LEFT" means "as opposed to right," but "LEFT TURN" is one sign.

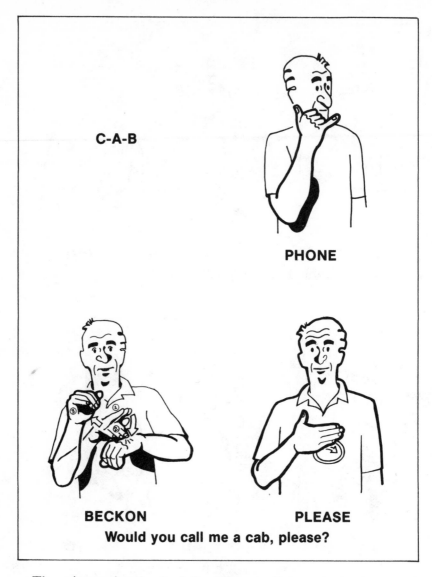

C-A-B

PHONE

BECKON   PLEASE

Would you call me a cab, please?

There is no sign for "cab," so fingerspell it at the beginning of the sentence, before the sign PHONE.

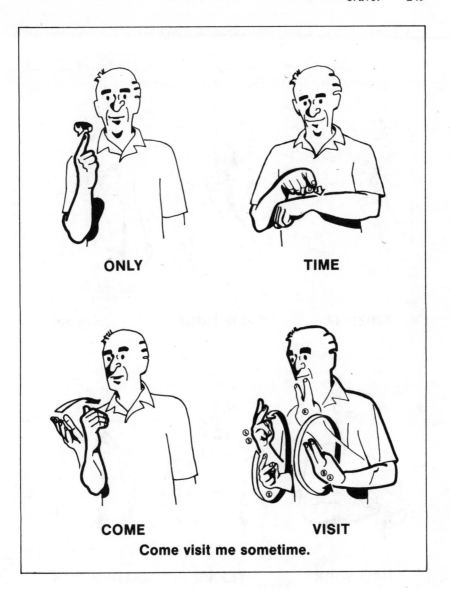

ONLY

TIME

COME

VISIT

Come visit me sometime.

Almost all states are fingerspelled using the standard written abbreviations such as Penn. or Pa., N.D., and Wyo. States such as Ohio that have short names are spelled out. The few states that have signs that are used throughout the country are shown below:

ARIZONA   **CALIFORNIA**   **HAWAII**

NEW YORK   **TEXAS**   **WASHINGTON**

14

Animals, Colors

ANIMALS

ASL does not have a sign for every animal. Presented here are nearly all the animal signs that do exist. All other animal names are either fingerspelled or have signs that are known only in a particular area.

ANIMAL   ALLIGATOR (1)   ALLIGATOR (2)

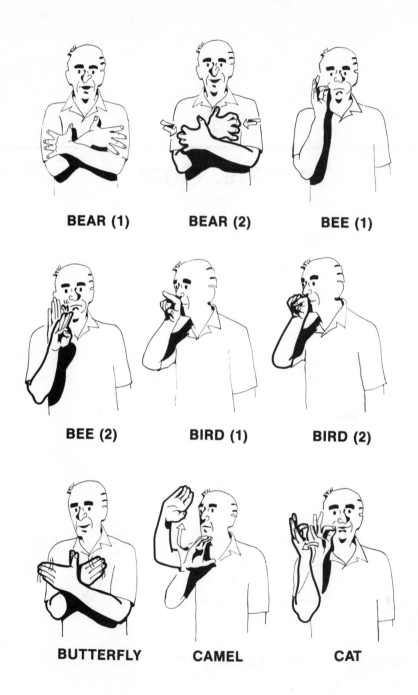

BEAR (1)   BEAR (2)   BEE (1)

BEE (2)   BIRD (1)   BIRD (2)

BUTTERFLY   CAMEL   CAT

CHICKEN* **COW** **DEER**

DOG **EAGLE** **ELEPHANT (A)**

ELEPHANT (B) **FROG** **GIRAFFE**

*While this sign means "chicken," the sign "BIRD" is also often used to mean "chicken."

GOAT   **HAWK**   **HORSE**

INSECT   **LION**   **MONKEY**

MOUSE   **MULE**   **RABBIT (A)**

RABBIT (B)   RAT   SHEEP

SNAKE   TIGER   WORM

TURKEY (A-1)   TURKEY (A-2)   TURKEY (B)

COLORS

ASL does not have a sign for every color, so "beige" and "fuchsia" have to be fingerspelled. Colors such as "blue-green," however, may be signed by combining the two signs BLUE and GREEN.

BLACK   BLUE   BROWN

GRAY (1)   GRAY (2)   GREEN

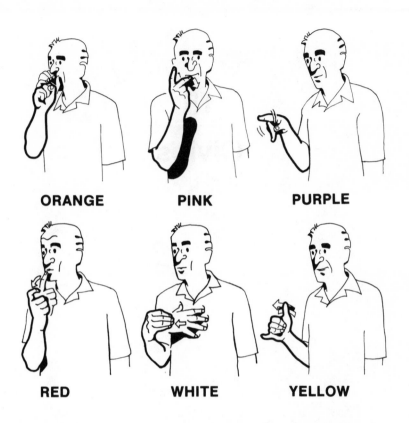

ORANGE **PINK** **PURPLE**

RED **WHITE** **YELLOW**

Varying shades of colors can be signed by using the signs DARK and CLEAR. In this sense, CLEAR means "light."

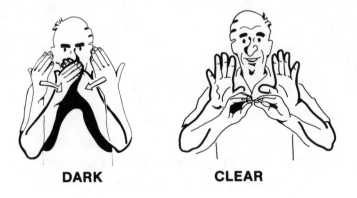

DARK **CLEAR**

15

Civics

DEMOCRAT   REPUBLICAN   INDEPENDENT   I
I'm a Democrat/Republican/Independent.

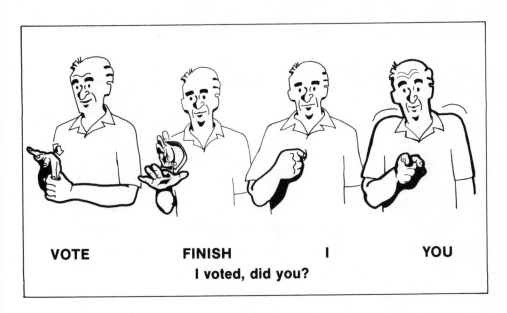

VOTE   **FINISH**   **I**   **YOU**

I voted, did you?

NEW   **PRESIDENT**   **WHO**

Who's the new president?

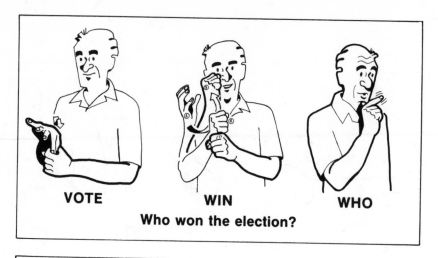

VOTE   **WIN**   **WHO**

Who won the election?

LAW   **PASS**   **RESPONSIBLE**

WHO   **LEGISLATURE**   **CONGRESS**

The legislature/congress is responsible for passing laws.

This is an example of the rhetorical question, where the signer asks, then answers, the question. It is used a great deal in ASL. There is a slight pause at the end of the question—after the sign WHO in this example—and then the answer is signed.

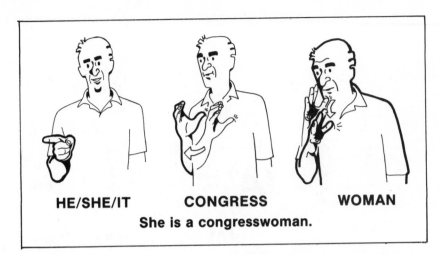

HE/SHE/IT   **CONGRESS**   **WOMAN**

She is a congresswoman.

The AGENT sign shown below is usually done following the SENATE, GOVERNMENT, JUDGE, and LAW signs to indicate senator, governor, judge, and lawyer, respectively. (See the discussion of the AGENT sign in the Dictionary/Index, page 327.)

HE/SHE/IT   **SENATE**   **GOVERNMENT**

JUDGE   **LAW**   **AGENT**

He is a senator/governor/judge/lawyer.

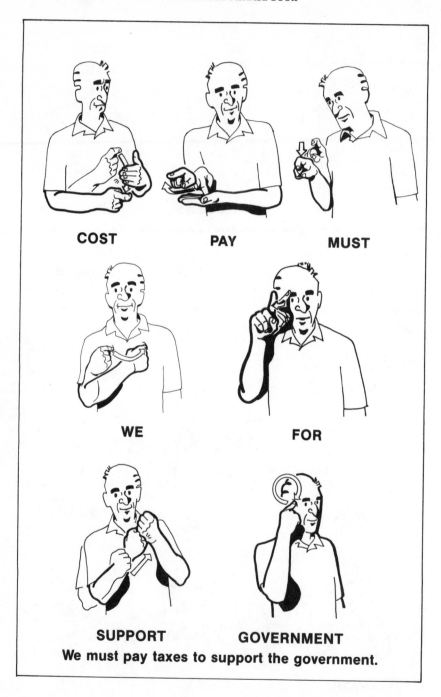

COST   PAY   MUST

WE   FOR

SUPPORT   GOVERNMENT

We must pay taxes to support the government.

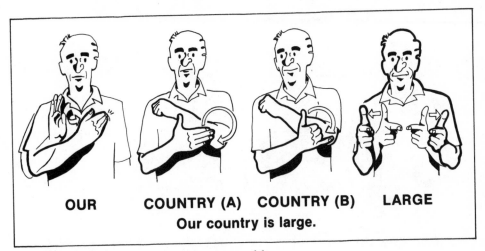

OUR   COUNTRY (A)   COUNTRY (B)   LARGE

Our country is large.

Either sign for "country" is acceptable.

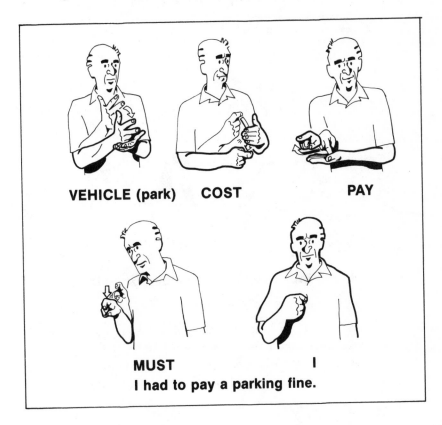

VEHICLE (park)   COST   PAY

MUST   I

I had to pay a parking fine.

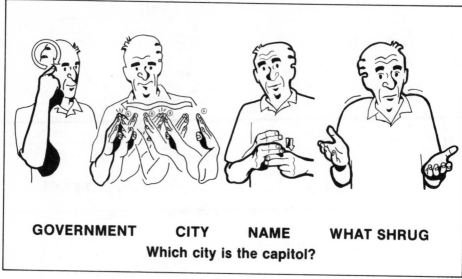

GOVERNMENT   CITY   NAME   WHAT SHRUG

Which city is the capitol?

LAW   BREAK   JAIL   MAYBE

If you break the law, you might go to jail.

The idea of "if" is often expressed in ASL by stating the sentence as a question. This requires a questioning expression. In the above sentence the expression would be done on the BREAK sign, and then there is a slight pause before you sign the consequence. In the following sentence, the questioning expression happens with the DISOBEY sign, which is followed by a pause before the rest of the statement is signed.

LAW   DISOBEY   PUNISH   WILL
If you disobey the law, you will be punished.

LAW   OBEY   MUST   YOU
You must obey the law.

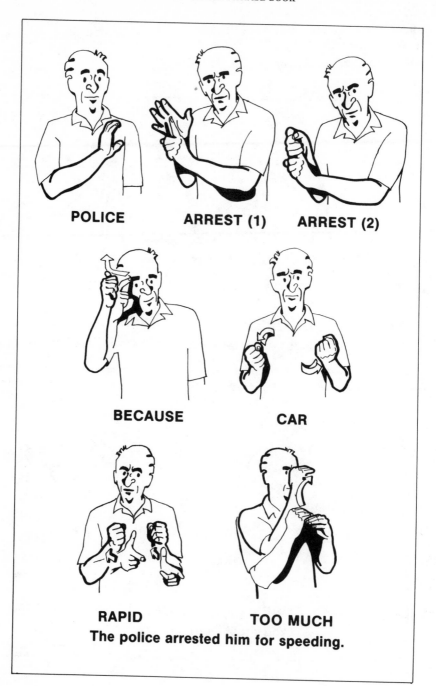

POLICE   ARREST (1)   ARREST (2)

BECAUSE   CAR

RAPID   TOO MUCH
The police arrested him for speeding.

HE/SHE/IT   **PLAN**   **AGAINST**
She plans to sue them.

THEY   **PROTEST**   **AGAINST**
They are on strike against the company.

There is no sign for "company," so fingerspell C-O at the end of the sentence after the sign AGAINST.

LAST YEAR   LEARN   AGENT   PROTEST

Last year the students protested.

PICKET   ALL MORNING   I

I was on the picket line all morning.

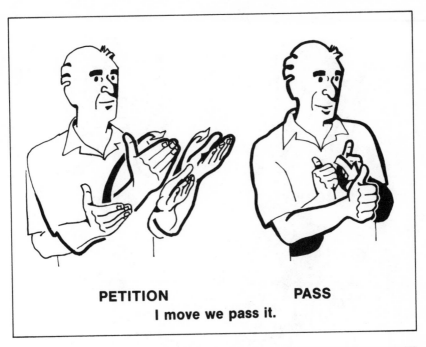

PETITION   **PASS**
I move we pass it.

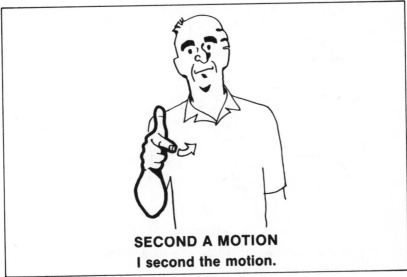

SECOND A MOTION
I second the motion.

This sign is also used idiomatically to show that you agree with someone.

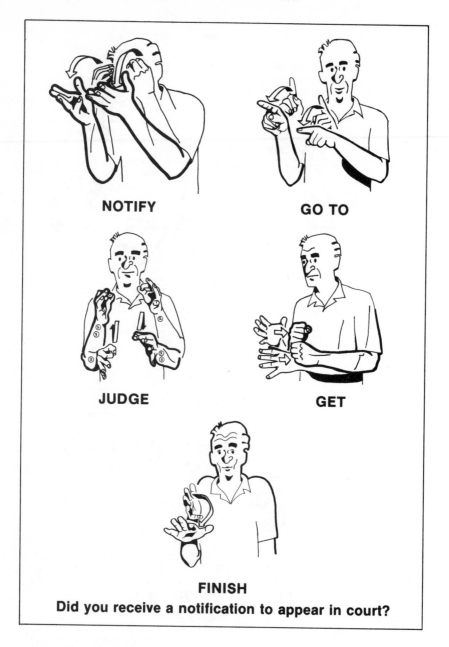

NOTIFY

GO TO

JUDGE

GET

FINISH

Did you receive a notification to appear in court?

P-T-A

JOIN   **YOU**

Do you belong to the P.T.A.?

There is no sign for "P.T.A.," so fingerspell it at the beginning of the sentence before the sign JOIN.

S-S

PENSION   **HE/SHE/IT**

He's on Social Security.

Fingerspell "S-S" to indicate "social security" at the beginning of the sentence before the sign PENSION.

S-S-I

PENSION   **HE/SHE/IT**

She gets Supplementary Salary Income.

Fingerspell "S-S-I" to indicate "Supplementary Salary Income" at the beginning of the sentence before the sign PENSION.

JUDGE   **GO TO**   **GOOD**

LAW   **AGENT**

MUST   **YOU**

If you go to court, you should have a good lawyer.

Do not forget the questioning facial expression, since this is an "if" statement. It should occur with the sign GO TO.

16

Religion

Signs for various denominations differ considerably around the country, so it is suggested that you make local inquiries about how specific denominations are signed in your area. Those that follow are fairly standard.

CHRIST   **AGENT**   **YOU**

Are you a Christian?

JEWISH   **OLD**   **RELIGION**

Judaism is an old religion.

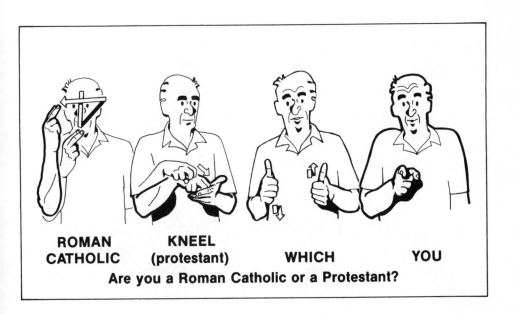

ROMAN CATHOLIC   **KNEEL (protestant)**   **WHICH**   **YOU**

Are you a Roman Catholic or a Protestant?

DISBELIEVE   **HE/SHE/IT**

He's an atheist.

BAPTIZE (Baptist)   **EPISCOPAL**

LUTHERAN   **MORMON**

BAPTIZE   **FINISH**   **YOU**

Have you been baptized?

If a particular denomination baptizes by sprinkling rather than by immersion, then one of the following signs is used:

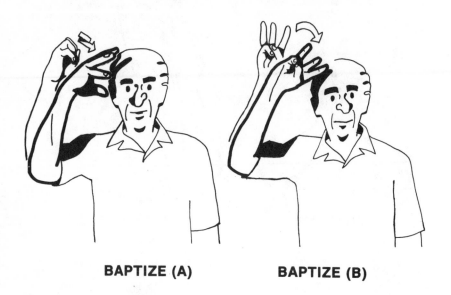

BAPTIZE (A)   **BAPTIZE (B)**

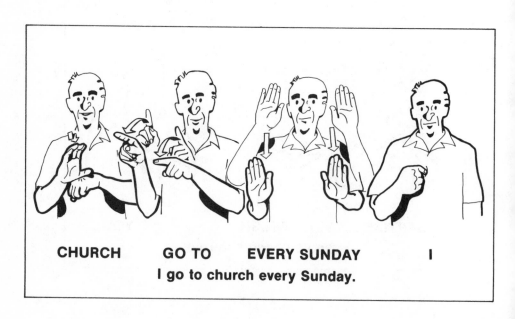

CHURCH   **GO TO**   **EVERY SUNDAY**   **I**

I go to church every Sunday.

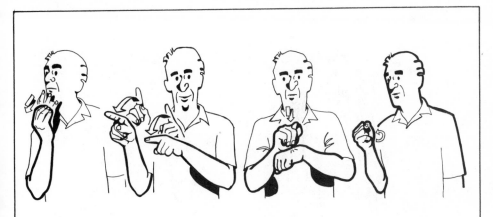

JEWISH   GO TO   TEMPLE   SATURDAY
Jewish people go to temple on the Sabbath.

CHURCH   JOIN   WHICH
Which church do you belong to?

LONG AGO   PREACH   HE/SHE/IT

He used to be a preacher.

MISSIONARY   HE/SHE/IT

She's a missionary.

ME

INTERPRET (1)

INTERPRET (2)

PREACH

WANT

YOU

Do you want me to interpret the sermon?

Additional vocabulary:

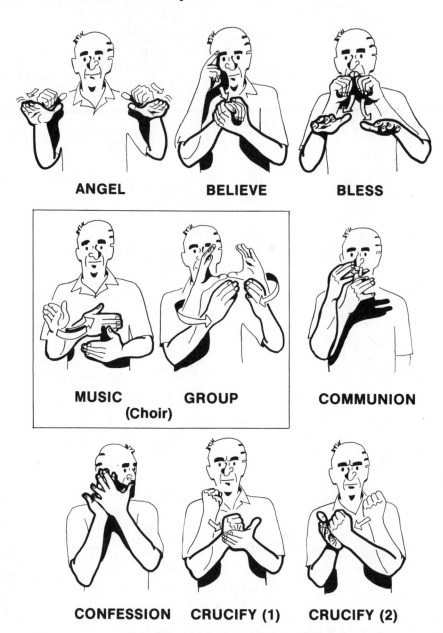

ANGEL   BELIEVE   BLESS

MUSIC   GROUP   COMMUNION
(Choir)

CONFESSION   CRUCIFY (1)   CRUCIFY (2)

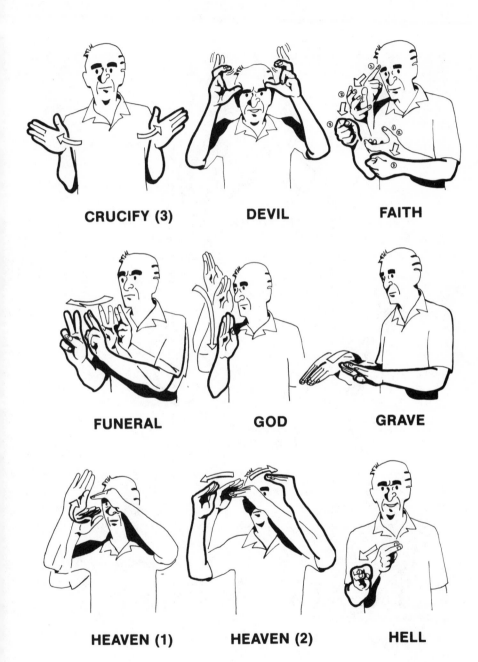

CRUCIFY (3)   DEVIL   FAITH

FUNERAL   GOD   GRAVE

HEAVEN (1)   HEAVEN (2)   HELL

JESUS (1)   **JESUS (2)**   **LORD**

MASS   **CRACKER**   **PITY**
               (Passover)

PRAY   **PRIEST**   **PROPHECY**

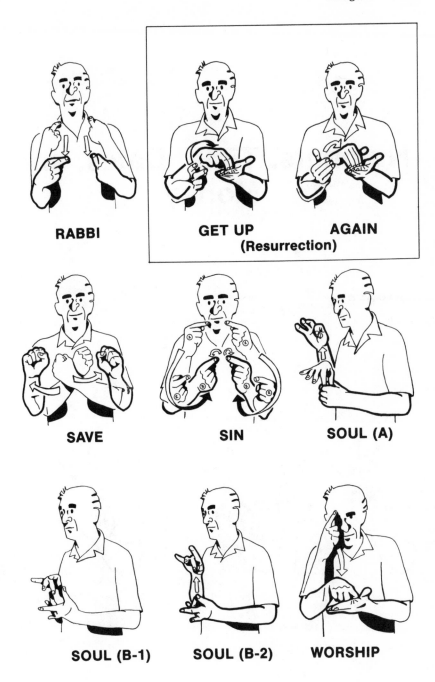

RABBI

GET UP
(Resurrection)

AGAIN

SAVE

SIN

SOUL (A)

SOUL (B-1)

SOUL (B-2)

WORSHIP

17

Numbers, Time, Dates, and Money

NUMBERS

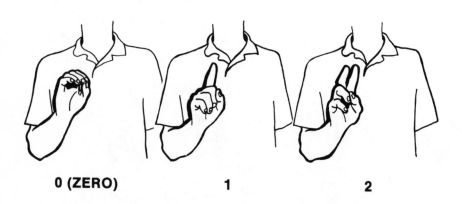

0 (ZERO)   1   2

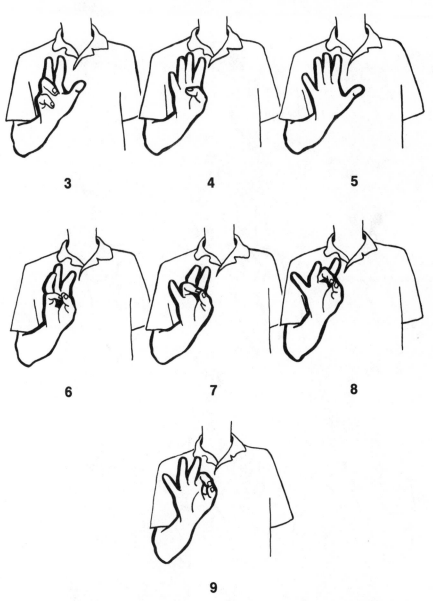

The signs for the number 6 and the letter W are exactly the same, and the sign for the number 9 is the same as that for the letter F. Context tells you whether the number or the letter is intended.

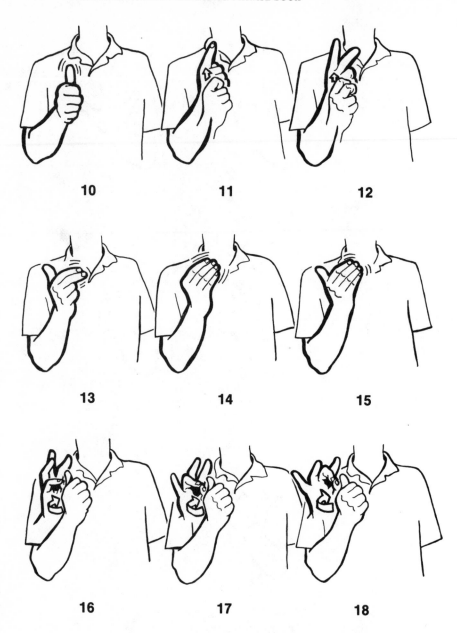

10

11

12

13

14

15

16

17

18

19

The numbers 16 through 19 are actually a very fast blend of 10 and 6, 10 and 7, 10 and 8, 10 and 9.

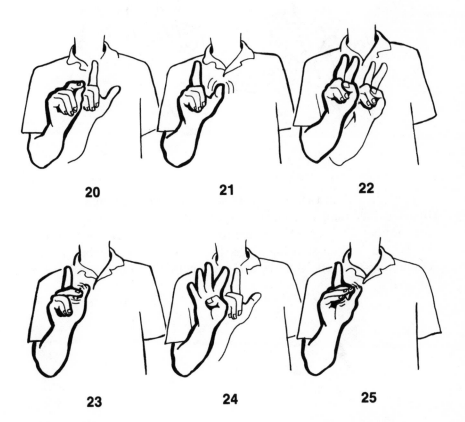

20   **21**   **22**

23   **24**   **25**

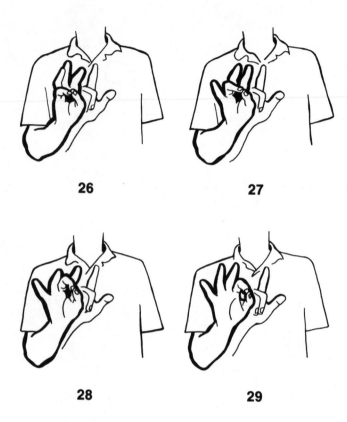

26   27

28   29

That the "2" in the twenties is made with the thumb and index finger rather than the index and second fingers—as it appears in the number 22—is probably due to the fact that ASL has its roots in the old French sign language. In Europe, even hearing people count *one* with the thumb, and *two* with the thumb and index finger.

The remaining numbers from 30 through 99 are done with the numbers 0 through 9. Examples follow:

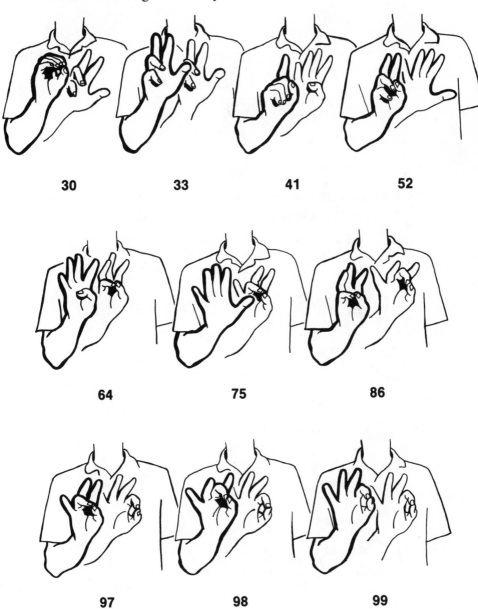

30	**33**	**41**	**52**

64	**75**	**86**

97	**98**	**99**

The number 100 is made by signing the number 1 and the letter C:

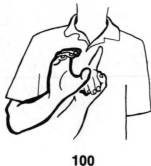

100

The numbers between 100 and 999 are made in one of two ways. One may make the number "7-7-7" or one may sign "7-C-7-7":

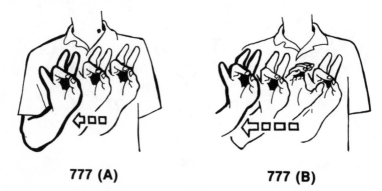

777 (A)   **777 (B)**

The numbers 1,000 and 1,000,000 are signed like so:

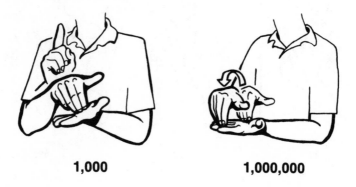

1,000   **1,000,000**

Fractions are made the same way they are written, one number above another:

½ **(A)**

The one-half sign as shown above is usually made more quickly as shown below:

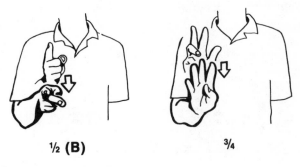

½ **(B)**　　　　　　　　　　³⁄₄

Percentages are made as follows:

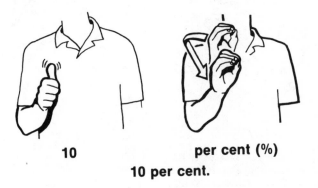

10　　　　　　　　**per cent (%)**
10 per cent.

Numbers with decimals can also be expressed:

1-.7-5
1.75

The sign for the decimal may also mean the punctuation mark "period."

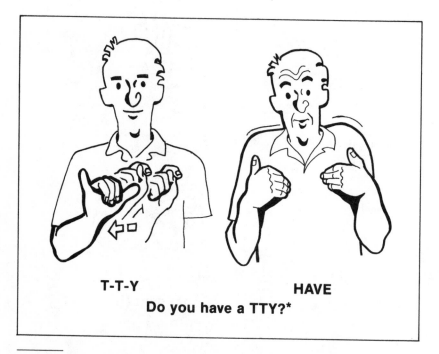

T-T-Y   **HAVE**
Do you have a TTY?*

---

*The TTY or TDD is a device that permits one to type messages back and forth over the telephone.

NUMBER   **WHAT**

What's your number?

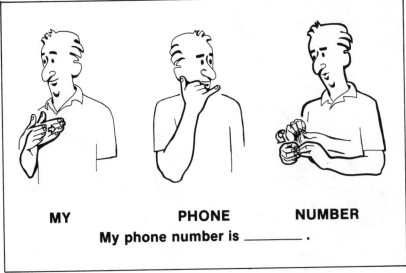

MY   **PHONE**   **NUMBER**

My phone number is _____ .

Fingerspell your phone number after the sign NUMBER.

TIME

Telling time in ASL is usually done exactly in the same way as it is done in English.

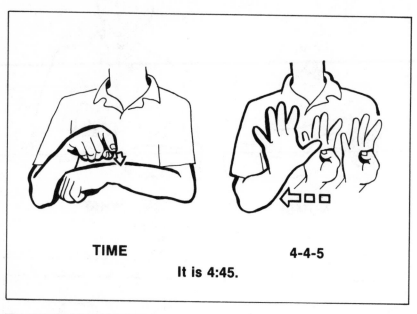

TIME   **4-4-5**

It is 4:45.

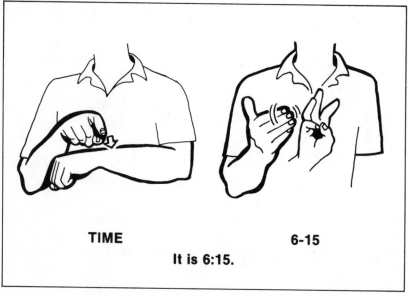

TIME   **6-15**

It is 6:15.

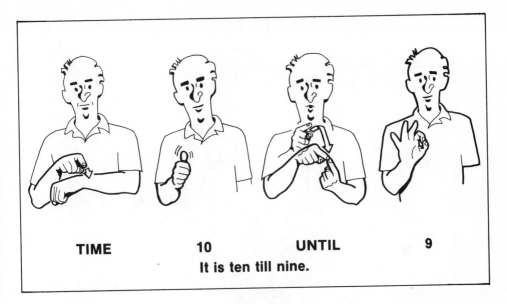

TIME   **10**   **UNTIL**   **9**

It is ten till nine.

DATES

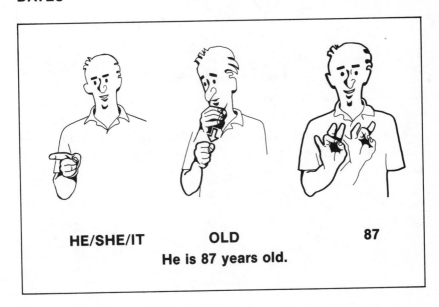

HE/SHE/IT   **OLD**   **87**

He is 87 years old.

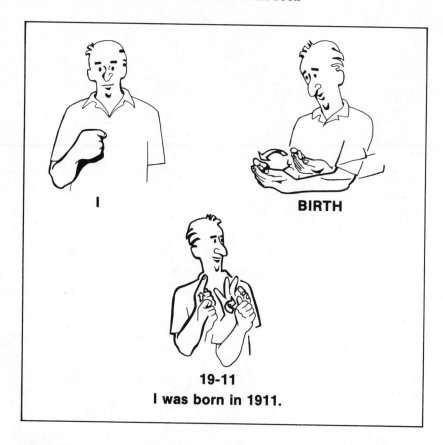

I

BIRTH

19-11
I was born in 1911.

Most of the months are abbreviated in fingerspelling. Only the short ones—March, April, May, June, and July— are spelled out completely.

MY

BIRTH

DAY

3

A-P-R-I-L

19-48

My birthday is April 3, 1948.

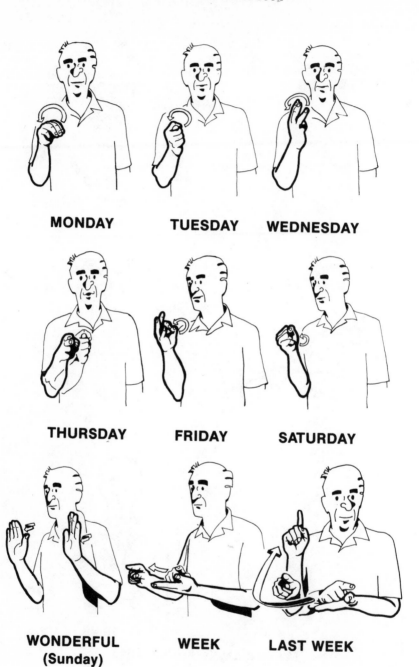

MONDAY   **TUESDAY**   **WEDNESDAY**

THURSDAY   **FRIDAY**   **SATURDAY**

WONDERFUL
(Sunday)   **WEEK**   **LAST WEEK**

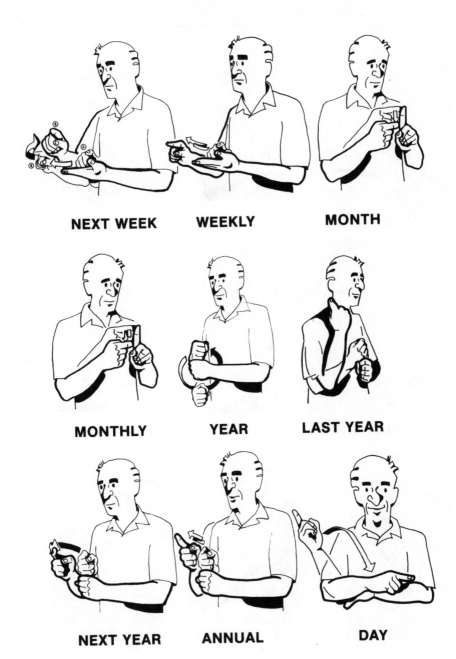

NEXT WEEK   **WEEKLY**   **MONTH**

MONTHLY   **YEAR**   **LAST YEAR**

NEXT YEAR   **ANNUAL**   **DAY**

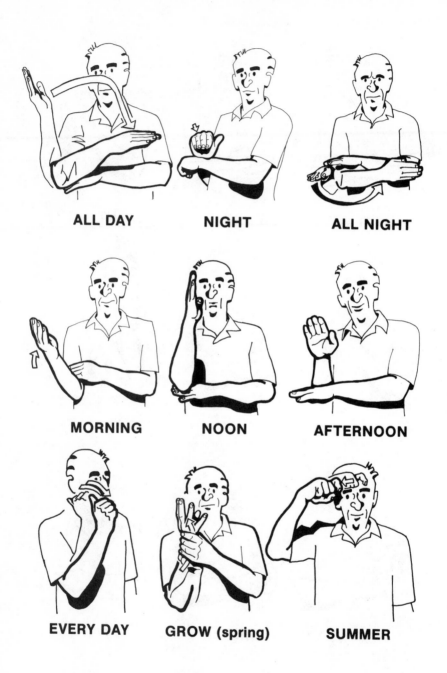

ALL DAY   NIGHT   ALL NIGHT

MORNING   NOON   AFTERNOON

EVERY DAY   GROW (spring)   SUMMER

AUTUMN

COLD (winter)

| SEE | NEAR FUTURE | MONDAY |

I'll see you next Monday.

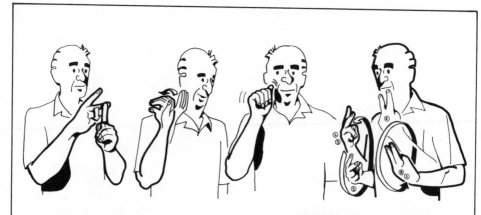

TWO MONTHS   PAST   AUNT   VISIT
I visited my aunt two months ago.

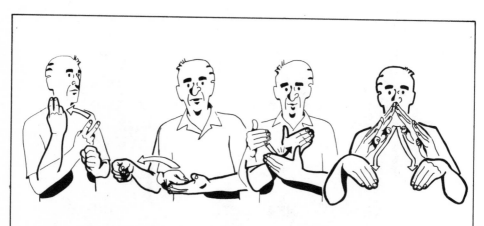

TWO YEARS AGO   BUY   NEW   HOUSE
I bought a new house two years ago.

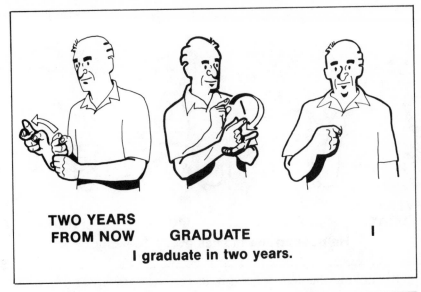

TWO YEARS FROM NOW   **GRADUATE**   **I**

I graduate in two years.

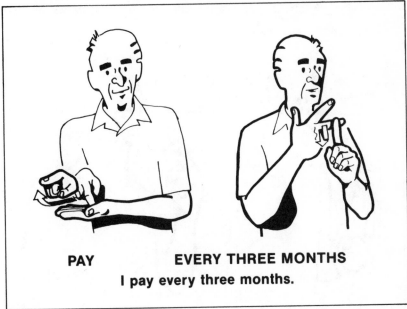

PAY   **EVERY THREE MONTHS**

I pay every three months.

**EVERY
TUESDAY**   **GO TO**   **MOVIE**   **HE/SHE/IT**

He goes to the movies every Tuesday.

By moving the sign for a day of the week downward, as done with TUESDAY here, you convey the idea of every week on that day.

EVERY SATURDAY   **SEE**

I see her every Saturday.

J-U-L-Y

4TH   **VACATION**

The fourth of July is a holiday.

Fingerspell JULY at the beginning of the sentence before the sign 4TH.

HAVE   **NICE**   **THANKSGIVING**   **THANKSGIVING**
                                         (1)   **(2)**

Have a nice Thanksgiving.

HAPPY   **CHRISTMAS**

Merry Christmas.

HAPPY   **HANUKKAH**

Happy Hanukkah.

HAPPY   NEW   YEAR
Happy New Year.

HAPPY   BIRTH   DAY
Happy birthday.

MONEY

These signs also serve as ordinal numbers—i.e., first, second, third, etc.

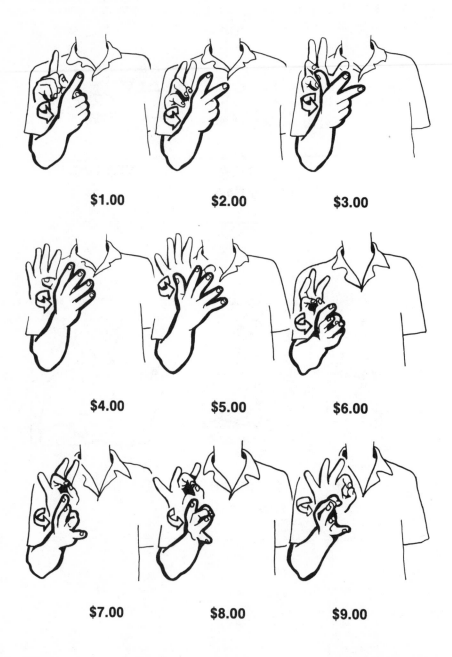

$1.00 $2.00 $3.00

$4.00 $5.00 $6.00

$7.00 $8.00 $9.00

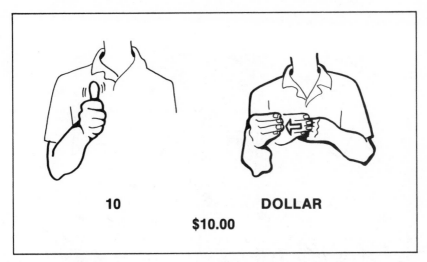

10

DOLLAR

$10.00

The sign DOLLAR is used when the amount is over nine dollars or when speaking specifically of a bill, as in "a dollar bill."

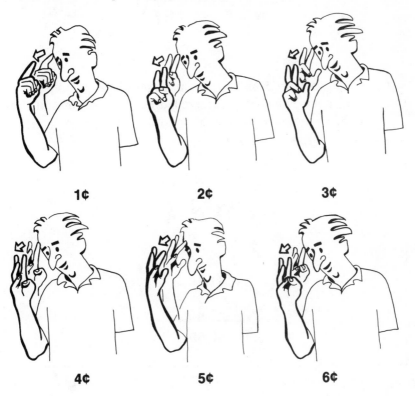

1¢   **2¢**   **3¢**

4¢   **5¢**   **6¢**

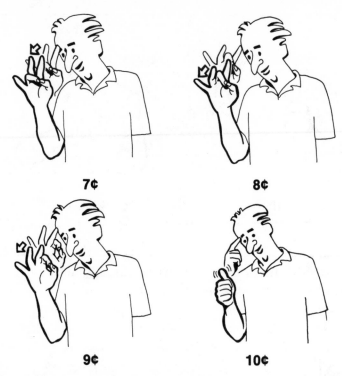

7¢   8¢

9¢   10¢

These signs are used only when speaking of these amounts by themselves, not when they are preceded by a dollar amount. For example, $3.09 would be signed as follows:

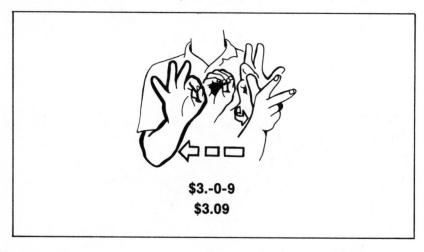

$3.-0-9
$3.09

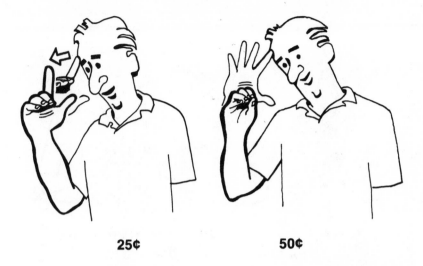

25¢   **50¢**

The same applies to these two signs as to the cent signs above. Use them only when speaking of these amounts alone, and not with a dollar amount.

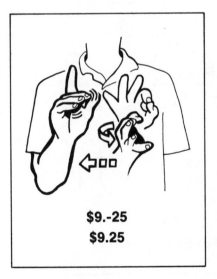

$9.-25
$9.25

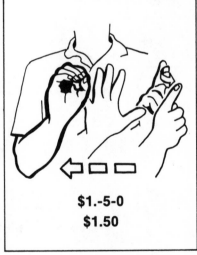

$1.-5-0
$1.50

BOOK   **COST**   **HOW MANY**

How much does the book cost?

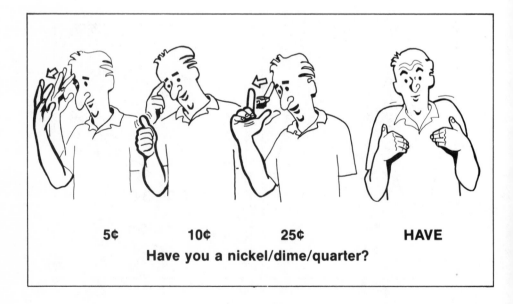

5¢   **10¢**   **25¢**   **HAVE**

Have you a nickel/dime/quarter?

$5.00 **SHARE (make change)** **CAN**
Can you change a five?

PAY **HOW MANY**
How much did you pay?

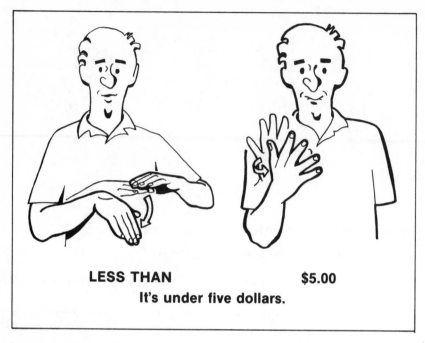

LESS THAN   **$5.00**

It's under five dollars.

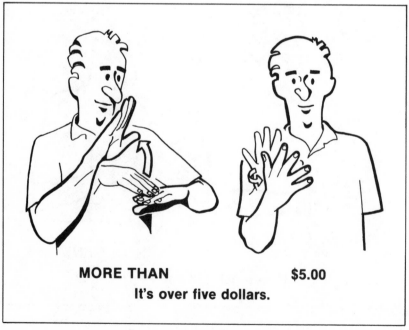

MORE THAN   **$5.00**

It's over five dollars.

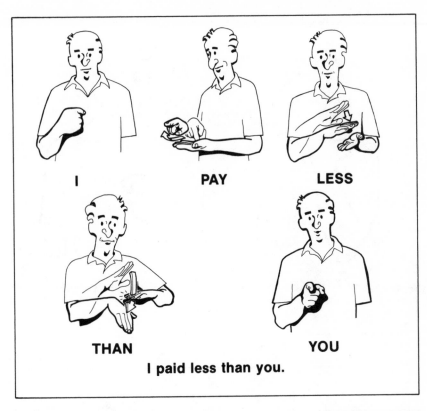

I   PAY   LESS

THAN   YOU

I paid less than you.

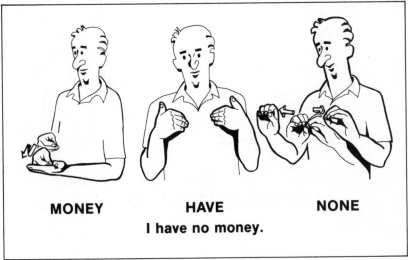

MONEY   HAVE   NONE

I have no money.

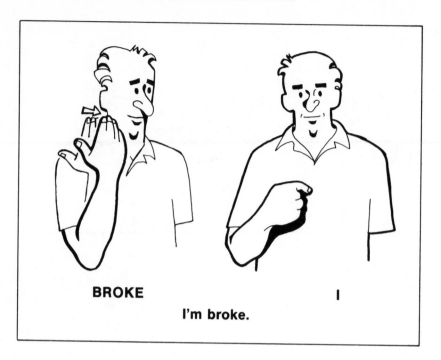

BROKE   **I**

I'm broke.

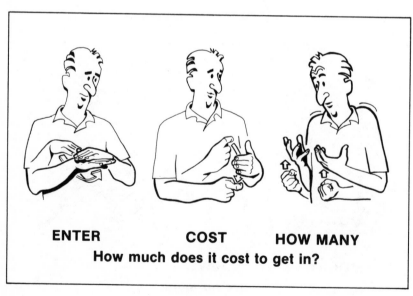

ENTER   **COST**   **HOW MANY**
How much does it cost to get in?

OWE   HOW MANY   HE
How much does he owe?

Appendix: The Manual Alphabet

The manual alphabet allows us to fingerspell English words. When there is not a sign for an idea, then fingerspelling is used. This occurs most often with proper names. Mastery of fingerspelling is relatively easy if you form good habits from the very beginning.

First, relax your fingers. This may require bending and stretching the fingers so that they fall easily into the proper hand shapes. Next, relax your arm and shoulder. Tension is the greatest obstacle to clear formation of the letters, so strive to remain relaxed as you work at it. Let the arm hang down with the elbow to your side and the hand slightly in front of your body as the pictures show. Do not let your elbow start moving away from your side and rising upwards.

Rhythm is the most important quality to develop in fingerspelling. A rhythmical spelling is much easier to read than an unrythmical one, even when the letters are not perfectly formed. Rhythm is also critical for indicating when one word has ended and the next word has begun. This is done by holding on to the last letter of a word for about one-fourth of a beat of the rhythm you are using, then going on to the first letter of the next word. As you practice rhythmical fingerspelling, be sure you do not let the rhythm cause you to bounce your hand. Hold it steadily in one place.

Speed is not a goal to pursue. Work on rhythm, and then speed will come naturally in time. The tendency is to attempt to finger-spell too fast. Then the rhythm becomes broken when you cannot remember how to make a letter. A slow, rhythmic pattern is far more desirable than a fast but erratic rhythm.

Do not say the letters, either aloud or to yourself, as you make them. This is a very bad habit to get into and exceedingly hard to break once established. As you fingerspell a word, say the whole word. For instance, as you spell "C-A-T" do not say the letters, but say the word "cat." You may say it aloud or without voice. It will seem awkward at first, but you will quickly become used to it.

The reason for speaking the word rather than saying the letters has to do with lipreading. Deaf people are taught to lipread words, not letters. When you fingerspell they see both your hand and your lips, and the two complement and reinforce each other. (This is also the reason you do not let your fingerspelling hand wander out to your side, too far away from your face.) It is not necessary to speak the word aloud; you may mouth it without using your voice.

When fingerspelling long words, pronounce the word syllable by syllable as you fingerspell it. For example, say, "fin" as you fingerspell "F-I-N," then say "ger" as you fingerspell "G-E-R," and then say "spell" as you fingerspell "S-P-E-L-L." (Double letters are moved slightly to the side or bumped back and forth slightly.) Caution: Do not pause after each syllable, but keep the rhythm flowing.

Practice spelling words, not just running through the alphabet. Begin with three-letter words, then work your way up to longer ones. A first-grade reading book provides excellent practice material because most of the words are short and are repeated often. Practice fingerspelling as you read a newspaper, listen to the radio or television, and see street signs and billboards. You may get some odd looks from some people, but never mind, you are on the road to mastering an intricate skill.

You will find that fingerspelling is much easier to do than to read. This happens because, initially, you tend to look for each individual letter as it is fingerspelled to you so that when you reach the end of the word you cannot make sense of the letters. You must learn to see whole words, not individual letters, just as you are doing as you read this printed material. You will have to find someone to learn and practice fingerspelling with you, since you cannot practice reading your own fingerspelling. As the two of you practice, do not speak or mouth the words since you would then hear or lipread them instead of reading the fingerspelling.

Here, in summary, are the tips to follow:
1. Relax.
2. Keep your elbow in and your hand in front of you.
3. Maintain a constant rhythm, but do not bounce your hand.
4. Pause for one-fourth of a beat at the end of each word.
5. Do not try to fingerspell rapidly.
6. Mouth or speak the word, not the letters.
7. Practice with someone so you can gain experience reading fingerspelling. (In this kind of practice, do not mouth or speak the word aloud.)
8. Look for the whole word, not individual letters.

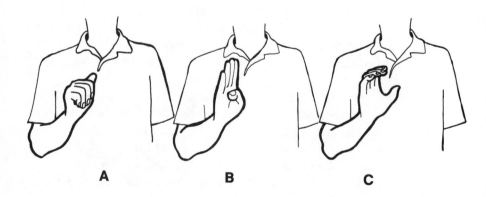

A   B   C

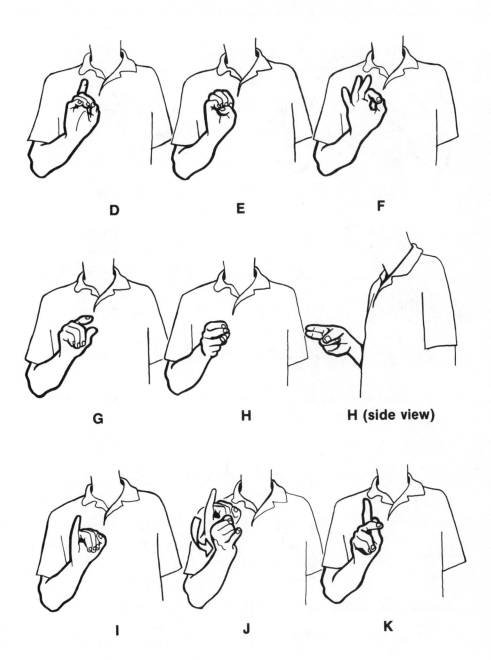

D   E   F

G   H   H (side view)

I   J   K

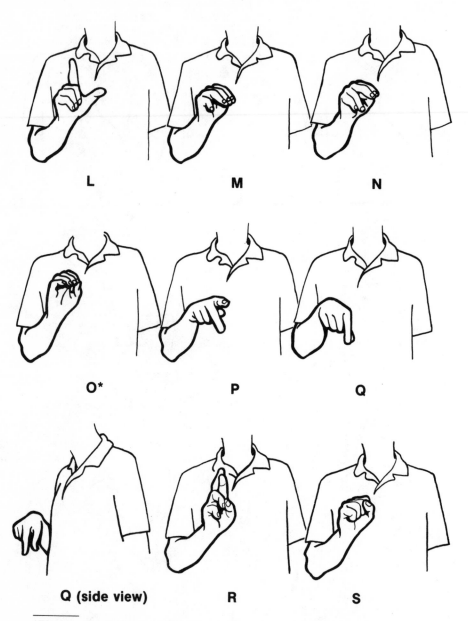

L   M   N

O*   P   Q

Q (side view)   R   S

*The sign for the letter "O" is the same as that for the number "0" (zero).

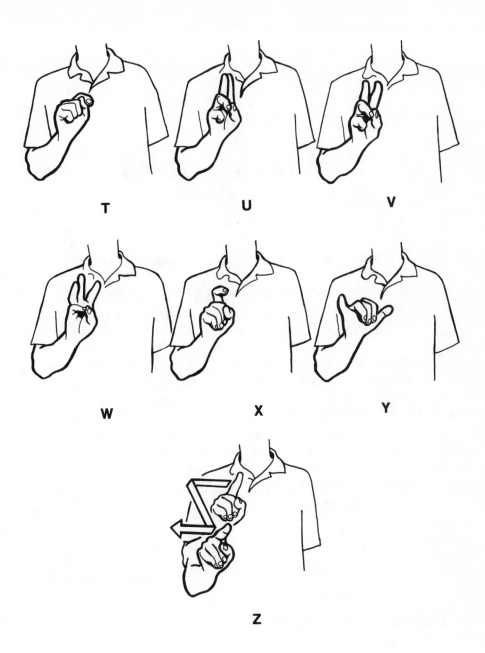

Dictionary/Index

The Dictionary/Index consists of a combination of three things:

1. All the signs in this book listed by sign labels. All sign labels are in capital letters. When the meaning of the sign is not evident from the sign label, additional definition and explanation are given.
2. English words that are glossed by signs in this book. The word is printed in lower-case letters, and the correct sign is in all capitals within parentheses following the word. Example: food (EAT). It is suggested that you refer to the sign label in the Dictionary/Index to see if additional definition or explanation is given before looking up the picture of the sign.
3. Topics that are discussed in various sections of this book. They are printed as titles. Examples: "Past, Present, Future"; "Labeling of the Drawings."

Abbreviations used:

SM = single movement. The movement of the sign is made only once.

DM = double movement. The movement of the sign is repeated once.

a lot of (MANY; MUCH) *118, 178*

ability (SKILL) *143, 218*

ABSENT *176*

ache (PAIN) *109, 112*

acquire (GET) *270*

ACT—actor/actress (also with the AGENT sign—optional); drama, play; theater *99, 158*

adapt (CHANGE) *235*

address (LIVE) *94, 146*

administer (CONTROL) *10, 164*

advice (ADVISE) *159*

ADVISE—counsel; guidance, advice; influence *159*

afraid (SCARE) *136*

AFRICA *225*

AFTERNOON *61, 135, 302*

after awhile (LATER) *64*

AGAIN—SM: over again, repeat *76;* DM: over and over

AGAINST—opposed to *267*

against the law (PROHIBIT) *169, 246*

age (OLD) *85, 104, 297*

AGENT—A sign used in conjunction with another sign in order to designate a person who does a particular thing. Example: AIRPLANE AGENT = pilot. *90, 99, 144, 145, 149, 161, 186, 261, 268, 273, 274*

ago (PAST) *14, 15, 30, 50, 51, 88, 119, 121, 131, 155, 216, 304*

AGREE—concur; agreement; fitting, appropriate, becoming *205*

aid (HELP) *38*

AIM—aspire, shoot for, hope to be; goal, objective *144*

AIRPLANE—SM: ride an airplane, fly *229;* DM: airplane; airport *149, 232, 234, 235, 236*

AIRPLANE—LANDING *240*

AIRPLANE—TAKE-OFF *233, 235*

ALL DAY *302*

all gone—(USED UP) *113*

ALL MORNING *268*

ALL NIGHT *166, 246, 302*

ALL RIGHT—be all right, be fine, be okay; it is all right; a civil right *67, 105, 108*

alike (SAME) *209*

ALLIGATOR *251*

already (FINISH) *4, 6, 31, 56, 57, 58, 119, 123, 137, 139, 150, 168, 175, 177, 188, 211, 229, 231, 238, 242, 259, 270, 277*

alter (CHANGE) *236*

although (BUT) *77, 216*

ALWAYS *204*

ambulance (EMERGENCY VEHICLE) *121*

AMERICA *226*

ANGEL *282*

Angle of the Pictures *12*

ANNUAL—every year, year after year *301*

ANIMAL—beast, creature *251*

Animals *251–55*

ANY *117, 174*

APPLE *192*

APPOINTMENT—reserve, reservation, engagement *122, 237*

appropriate (AGREE) *205*

approve (SECOND MOTION) *269*

THAT—This sign can mean: this, that, them, those, they, and it. Idiomatically it can mean, "Oh, I see," "So, that's it," or "Ah, ha, I get it!" It is often done by the watcher while the signer is